D. H. Lawrence in Italy

D. H. Lawrence
in Italy

LEO HAMALIAN

TAPLINGER PUBLISHING COMPANY

NEW YORK

First printing
First published in 1982 by
TAPLINGER PUBLISHING CO., INC.
New York, New York

LIBRARY OF CONGRESS CATALOGING IN PUBLICATION DATA
Hamalian, Leo.
D. H. Lawrence in Italy.

Bibliography: p.
Includes index.
    1. Lawrence, D. H. (David Herbert), 1885–
1930—Homes and haunts—Italy. 2. Lawrence,
D. H. (David Herbert), 1885-1930—Biography.
3. Italy—Description and travel—1901-1944.
4. Italy in literature. 5. Authors, English—
20th century—Biography. I. Title
PR6023.A93Z63123   823'.912   [B]   81-50226
        ISBN 0-8008-4572-2   AACR2

designed by GANIS & HARRIS, INC.

Contents

Preface

A restless spirit in quest of permanency, D. H. Lawrence moved from place to place carrying his belongings in two suitcases, a steamer trunk, and a knapsack on his back. I tried to follow in his Italian footsteps, and visiting the various places where he had lived or stayed proved to be helpful when I needed to establish the precise setting for one of his works or when I wanted to identify people he had used as raw material for his fiction. Moreover, the visual experience enabled me to appreciate that special aura associated with his descriptive writing, something he himself called "the spirit of place."

In gathering material for this study, I talked or corresponded with people who knew Lawrence a little or well: among them were Ezechiele Azzanini, Dorothy Brett, Caresse Crosby, Marrucia Cervi, Cicio Cacopardo, Yvonne Franchetti Hamilton, Enid Hilton, Maria Ferraro, Jan Juta, Raul Mirenda, Eric Quayle, Angelo Ravagli, Dorothy Yorke, members of the Fasola and Petterich families, and Percy Lubbock and his family. Harry Moore gave me many useful leads. I wish they were all alive to see their contributions to this book.

In a book intended for the general rather than the special reader, it would have been inappropriate to encumber the text with complete annotations and references. I did, however, provide footnotes when certain information would have clogged the flow of narrative if left in the text. And for anyone who wishes to know more about the sources I consulted, there is a selected bibliography drawn from the formidable accumulation of Lawrence criticism, biography, and scholarship (after Joyce, Lawrence is the most commented-upon writer of our time). And this is the place for me to say that it was impossible to acknowledge every debt that I owe to others—much of it has melted into my unconscious memory—though my dependence upon Warren Roberts and Edward Nehls in particular must be evident throughout the book.

Since this is a sympathetic account of Lawrence's years in Italy, his experience there is seen largely through his own eyes. This means that an incomplete image is often given of other people who enter into the account. Also, not all readers may agree with the interpretation of Lawrence that emerges from these pages. Indeed, some readers may discover a Lawrence quite different from the one they had imagined or the one familiar to them through other accounts.

I wish to thank Richard Balkin and Samuel Lawrence for their encouragement during the various stages of this book. And I am deeply grateful to my wife Linda for her attentive reading and her steady support when my own interest in the book was diverted. And I am thankful for the patient, wise, and sympathetic reading of my editor and copy editor at Taplinger Publishing Co. Whatever infelicities or errors may have escaped their eagle eyes are purely my own fault.

Leo Hamalian

Introduction

When Goethe first arrived in Rome, he exclaimed: *"Nun bin ich endlich geboren!"* ("At last I am born!"). Entering Italy in 1913, D. H. Lawrence could have said the same. It was in Italy that he found the essence of his being, and as we read the prose, poetry, and correspondence associated with his years in Italy, we can begin to appreciate the profound influence and rejuvenating effect that this place and people had upon his creative powers.

Though he wearied of Italy near the end of his life, no other land could have suited the temperament of the young writer so well. Germany, where he thought to live, got on his nerves very soon: he fumed over German stupidity when he was almost arrested for allegedly spying; and the Rhine Valley countryside he regarded as "rather pretty in a tame sort of way." And he could not abide a nation of people who spoke "an atrocious language."

Switzerland, the favorite haunt of English expatriates in Lawrence's time, swarmed with tourists, and the vaunted scenery Lawrence found "so ordinary that it was . . . soul-killing." The Norwegians and Swedes, he feared, might be detestable, "fingering with the mind the secret places and sources of the blood, impertinent, irreverent, nasty," making of the phallus an unclean fetish. Austria had invigorating summers and unspoiled peasants. But the severe winters, he thought, might tax his health; furthermore, the manners of the Tyrolese reminded him of chocolate soldiers, and in spirit, they seemed "too introspective and self-conscious." France was too prosperous and Spain too impoverished for Lawrence.

Italy, on the other hand, represented Europe as it stood at a great point of opposition to the temperament of northern Europe. The Italian attitude toward the dictates of passion was tolerant and subtle, and Lawrence, weary of English inhibition, felt that he could happily adjust to this less frigid psychological (as well as geographical) climate. Lawrence wanted to live among people connected to a civilization which respected the elemental powers of human nature. Italy, he believed, would provide a hospitable space where both the light and dark gods of his imagination, in communion or in conflict, might thrive and develop without tether.

Furthermore, Italy had a kind of natural magic. When Lawrence first crossed its northern frontier about seventy years ago, the physical attractions of Italy had not yet been diminished by modern industry and tourism. Italians were unspoiled by war and commerce. A traveler like Lawrence approaching from the north was transported into a different world, a world which his readers may experience vicariously through his fiction, poetry, travel books, and letters (Lawrence raised the last two into art forms).

It is probably significant that Lawrence and Frieda chose to live in villages and isolated places, rather than in the large cultural centers of Italy. The countryside suggested the possibility of profound mysteries: for Lawrence, it was associated with the ancient civilizations of the Mediterranean; it represented a continuity with an older, wiser way of life, increasingly appealing as the present became increasingly appalling. Though he loved its monuments of splendor and its works of art, Italy meant more to Lawrence than museums and galleries: above all, it meant a land of legend allied to a special destiny, with a history that stretched back to the dawn of time.

Thus, Italy was a symbol. It was a spirit, an *anima*, a way of life; it was sunshine and sensitivity and passion: it was all these things in harmony with a people of living flesh and blood who clung to these values in spite of everything. It was the Italy of Lawrence's imagination that helped him to resolve his soul-tearing conflicts and to affirm the future by a creative exploration of the past. Italy was, in brief, the inspiration of his visionary quest.

PART I

Flight to Italy

(September 1912–June 1914)

Chapter 1

WHY D.H. Lawrence, recognized as a promising young writer by literary critics and men of letters, decided to leave England for Italy is made abundantly clear by the course that both his personal and professional life had taken. His mother had died in 1910, an event whose full emotional impact he would recall in *Sons and Lovers*: "The world began to dissolve around me, beautifully iridescent, but passing away substanceless. Till I almost dissolved away myself and was very ill." Paul's "drift towards death" was his own.

In the unusually cruel winter of 1911, his defenses further reduced by a persistent cold, D. H. Lawrence contracted pneumonia for the third time and had to leave the Davidson Road School in Croydon, where he had been teaching an upper class at one hundred pounds per annum. This brief career of three years seems to provide no grounds for T. S. Eliot's snide remark that frightful consequences might have ensued if Lawrence "had been a don at Cambridge, rotten and rotting others." His absence from school was prolonged by neuritis of the leg. Even though by February of 1912 he seemed to be recovered, he remarks to a colleague, "I don't think I want to return to Davidson," and a month later, he writes to Edward Garnett, "In May I go to Germany, God speed the day." In March, he made up his mind. Shocked to learn that a colleague had died of the illness to which he himself was so susceptible, he officially resigned from the position which he felt was draining him physically and spiritually. His mood of that period is reflected in a letter to Helen Corke, a beloved friend and fellow teacher in south London: "the one beautiful and generous adventure left seemed to be death."

Less than a month later, this bleak mood was to brighten. Possibly because his aunt Ada and her husband, Professor Fritz Krenkow, the distinguished Orientalist, were living in Germany, Lawrence thought he might apply for an English lectureship at one of the universities there. He decided to seek advice from Ernest Weekley, a favorite professor at the University of Nottingham, who had studied abroad and had married a German woman. He walked the eight miles to Nottingham and called upon the Weekleys. Despite the difference in age and background, he found himself drawn to Weekley's wife, Frieda—whom he may have met earlier in Eastwood—and fascinated by her accounts of her youth as a von Richthofen. Frieda fell in love with the English visitor.

Thereafter, they cooperated in kitchen chores and conversed long and frequently. No doubt Lawrence told his sympathetic listener about his aspirations as a struggling artist—his love of painting; a play called *A Collier's Friday Night* (which was to remain unpublished until after his death); the stories and poems which had appeared in Ford Madox Hueffer's *The English Review,* then the best publication in England; a first novel called *The White Peacock* and a second in manuscript, *The Trespasser,* about a young woman and the father of three children who came to grief because they break off a love affair and try to pursue their old lives. Impressed by his imagination and touched by his tenderness, Frieda invited him to sleep with her one day while her husband was away, but Lawrence (so says Frieda), instead of leaping into bed, persuaded her to tell her husband the truth upon his return.

The couple soon discovered that the English were not disposed to be friendly toward an illicit liaison. Lawrence knew they would be ostracized if they were to remain in England. Furthermore, Lawrence was already chafing under the restraints of those whom he later characterized as "the censor-morons," and his experience with the first two novels foreshadowed storms to break. *The White Peacock* was published in England by Heinemann from the plates of the American publisher, Duffield. Heinemann asked Lawrence to rewrite a paragraph which they felt might be considered objectionable.

The Trespasser, completed shortly before Lawrence met Frieda, was accepted for publication by Heinemann, but Hueffer, then reading for the firm, expressed the opinion that it was "a rotten work of genius . . . execrably bad art" as well as "erotic." Piqued, Lawrence withdrew the novel and even agreed with Hueffer's prediction that its eroticism could permanently damage his future reputation, until Edward Garnett, who had read the manuscript for Duckworth, encouraged Lawrence to revise the book. Lawrence did so and published with Duckworth.

In 1912, Lawrence returned to Eastwood. The colliery where his father worked was struck. The suffering caused by the unemployment depressed Lawrence and he wrote: "I hate Eastwood abominably, and I should be glad if it were puffed off the face of the earth." By the end of April he says to Frieda: "I feel as if I can't breathe while we're in England."

Lawrence had already accepted an invitation to visit the Krenkows in Waldbröl (eighty miles from Trier), and Frieda had been planning to visit her parents in Metz for the fiftieth "jubilee" of her father's commission into the army. One night early in May the couple slipped onto the night ferry at Dover, and "sitting on the ropes, full of hope and agony," crossed a gray sea to Ostend. In the "continental" chapter of *Women in Love*, Birkin and Ursula make a strikingly similar crossing of the Channel to Ostend ("Birkin found a comparatively sheltered nook, where a great rope was coiled up. . . . Here they sat down, folded together, folded round with the same rug . . .") and a similar "wild long journey" to Metz by train. Whereas the fictional twosome would continue on to Basle, Lawrence and Frieda stayed in Metz at the Hotel Deutscher Hof—in separate quarters, a practice they were not to abandon altogether. Lawrence immediately dispatched a letter to Weekley which sealed the situation. Frieda and Lawrence had turned their backs on their old secure ways and had taken up the life of exile.

Lawrence left Frieda in Metz to spend an interlude with the Krenkows in Waldbröl. One of his letters to her proved useful to him fifteen years later at Scandicci, when he was completing *Lady Chatterley's Lover*. Mellors writes a letter to Constance which describes his precarious situation in words almost precisely parallel to the ones below:

> Do tell me if you can what is Ernest's final decision. He will get the divorce, I think . . . and then after six months, we will be married—will you? We must decide what we are going to do, very definitely. If I am to come to Munich next week, what are we going to live on? . . . If we can go decently over the first three or four months—financially—I think I shall be able to keep us going for the rest. Never mind about the infant. If it should come, we will be glad, and stir ourselves to provide for it—and if it should not come, ever—I shall be sorry.

Toward the end of May, Lawrence rejoined Frieda, and they stayed briefly in the nearby village of Icking, where the resourceful Frieda had procured, probably through the good offices of her sister, Frau Else Jaffe-Richthofen, the apartment belonging to Else's lover, Dr. Alfred Weber, the political scientist and brother of Max Weber, while he was up at Heidelberg. Lawrence wrote glowingly to Garnett, his chief confidant of this period, about that idyllic interlude in Bavaria: about bathing naked in the "quick stream" of the Isar, hiking through the flowering hills and battening on love despite an occasional spat ("Love rather suits me. I am getting fat and look awfully well").

This buoyant mood was marred by the news that Frieda's divorce might be delayed indefinitely and by "storms of letters from England [presumably from Weekley, their children, and Nottingham friends] imploring her to renounce for ever her ideas of love" (letter to Garnett, July 3, 1912). When Frieda seemed indecisive, Lawrence told her: "Decide what you want most, to live with me and share my rotten chances, or to go back to security, and your children—decide for *yourself*—choose for yourself." Frieda went off for four days to look after her sister's children, and Lawrence fired off this salvo to Garnett:

> Why, who and why was I born an Englishman!—my cursed rottenboned, puppy hearted countrymen, *why* was I sent to *them*. Christ on the cross must have hated his countrymen. 'Crucify me, you swine,' he must have said through his teeth. . . .

This was not the last time that Lawrence's imagination was to be inflamed by the image of himself as the suffering Christ—the sight of the Son of Man, in visage curiously resembling his own, crucified in carved wood, displayed everywhere in the small churches and wayside shrines of Bavaria and the Tyrol, must have fed his conviction that he was being martyred. Shortly after this outburst, he distilled his impressions of the Tyrolean crucifixes into the famous essay that opens *Twilight in Italy*, "The Crucifix Across the

Mountains" (in the original version called "Christs in the Tirol"), and in the conclusion to *Women in Love*, he used the scene of the crucifix in the snow symbolically to suggest that the ungenial Gerald in his last mad moments had associated his sufferings with those of Christ—perhaps an indication that Christ figures in Lawrence come in several varieties. When he began to paint years later in Florence, the memory of the crucifixes stirred his imagination, and those stark, suffering faces emerged softened and eroticized on his canvases. In his writing the same kind of transformation appears in one of his most original short novels, *The Man Who Died*.

But at that moment, he was preoccupied with other thoughts. The critical reception to his flight with Frieda hardened his determination to become an exile and, despite all opposition, to hold on to her (*"I loathe Paul Morel,"* he said, referring no doubt to Paul's indecisiveness). In July of 1912, he wrote to Edward Garnett:

> There is talk of getting me some lecturing in München for the winter. I dread it a bit. Here, in this tiny savage little place, F. and I have got awfully wild. I loathe the idea of England . . . I don't want to go back to town and civilisation.

When no teaching possibilities developed, Lawrence and Frieda decided to spend the winter in the milder climate of Italy, either at Lake Garda or Lake Maggiore. With only twenty-three pounds in his pocket, Lawrence chose the less fashionable lake. In August, he and Frieda walked to Mayrhofen in Austria, and there were joined by David Garnett, Edward Garnett's son, and Harold Hobson, the son of the social economics writer, John Atkinson Hobson. The four of them crossed the Alps via the Brenner Pass. "The Crucifix Across the Mountains," records the Lawrences' impressions of this walk, and slightly fictionalized accounts of episodes from the same journey appear in *Love Among the Haystacks*, a collection of previously rejected pieces published posthumously in 1930. The preface by David Garnett contains a lively portrait of Lawrence brimming with humor and joy.

Lawrence and Frieda continued at a leisurely pace until they came to Riva, at the head of Lake Garda, a place which Lawrence described as "quite beautiful and perfectly Italian." For two weeks they stayed at a *pensione* called the Villa Leonardi, house hunting when they were not hiking to nearby cities like Meran, Bozen ("beautiful but beastly"), and Trient ("pure Italian ancient decrepit"). Lawrence was beginning to learn a little Italian and to write again, working over the last section of *Sons and Lovers* (which was originally called "Paul Morel") and polishing up some poems later to appear in *Amores* and in *Look! We Have Come Through!*

In mid-September, they took the steamer to Torbole, a few kilometers east of Riva, to look at a "red place" that Frieda liked. It proved to be already rented. When Frieda inquired of a passerby (*"Prego . . . Herr . . . Herr . . . quartiere . . . d'affittare"*) he suggested that they take the afternoon steamer and try Gargnano, about twenty kilometers from Riva on the Brescia side of the lake. At Gargnano, the proprietress of the Hotel Cervo introduced them to a "little shrivelled man, with close-cropped grey hair on his skull, and a protruding jaw who could speak a broken French" (Lawrence has a splendid portrait of him in "The Lemon Gardens" of *Twilight in Italy*). Signor Pietro di Paoli owned a little villa with a furnished apartment to let: a dining room, a kitchen with a large open fireplace, two sunny bedrooms looking toward the lake, a courtyard, and a garden, for about eighty lire a month (three guineas or about fifteen dollars in those days). It was, according to the owner, as clean as a flower.

The house, which was called the Villa Igéa (with an accent over the *e* for the benefit of foreigners), occupies number 44

on the Via Calleta, a narrow dirt lane leading out of the
town square, and looks today as it did in Lawrence's time:
surrounded by rosebushes, persimmon, fig, peach, bamboo,
and especially lemon trees, and adjoined by a small plot of
cultivated land, it enjoys quiet privacy and a breeze from the
dark purple waters of Garda. Inasmuch as Lawrence had just
received an unexpected windfall of fifty pounds from Duckworth and found the apartment quite charming, he accepted
it without the usual formality of haggling over price. Within
a week, Signor di Paoli was sending Frieda and Lawrence
baskets of figs and grapes and asking Lawrence to fix the
latch spring of a miscreant door. The couple were comfortably installed in their first home.

Lake Garda is the ancient Lacus Benacus sung by Virgil
and Pliny. The northern end is hemmed by mountains while
the southern part resembles a small inland sea. Sheltered
from the cold winds of the north, it enjoys a temperate
climate and is surrounded by splendid vegetation: the famous vines of Bardolino, groves of lemon trees, stands of
palms, oleander, and venerable cypresses. Though the
southern and western shores of the lake are now overrun by
tourists and pizza parlors, one can understand why Catullus
came to Sermione to soothe his annoyance over the in-
fidelities of Lesbia. Across the lake under the shadow of
Monte Baldo, Goethe was held prisoner in 1786 at the Palace
of the Captains for making a sketch of the castle. At Gar-
done Riviera, about five miles south of Gargnano, Gabriele
D'Annunzio built himself an estate known as the Vittoriale,
and Maurice Barrès, the French novelist and nationalist, was
one among several writers before Lawrence who also succumbed to the attractions of Lake Garda.

In those days, there were hardly any "resorts" on the lake,
and no motorboats towing water skiers churned over its
surface. But the lake was dotted by fishing smacks with
lemon-colored sails, from a distance looking completely

motionless, or if the morning fog had not yet risen, seeming to float on the mists. Occasionally one caught sight of the steamer going down the lake to Desenzano.

Gargnano itself was a "tumbledown Italian place straggling along the lake . . . only accessible by steamer." The narrow old Church of San Tommaso with its "Jacob's ladder of steps" rose sheer above *la bella strada militaire* (now a modern highway so full of tourist traffic that one does not recognize Lawrence's description of it in *Twilight in Italy*). In the village below, peasants led their oxen carts along the cobbled, submerged streets and fishermen repaired their nets in the dark little square where was hidden the Church of San Francesco, "its pink walls . . . blind, windowless, unnoticeable."

To this natural magic Lawrence submitted immediately, and in this serene setting and kindly atmosphere he found the leisure and freedom that he craved. During the winter of 1912 and the spring of 1913, the happiest period of Lawrence's career, his mood was often joyful, and sometimes in a rather unjovial way, even jolly. He writes to Ernest Collings, an artist friend: "I live in sunshine and happiness, in exile and poverty, here in this pretty hole," and to Edward Garnett, "This is one of the most beautiful countries in the world. You must come. Life is simple and beautiful." Now he depicts himself scrubbing floors for Frieda, then helping her to grate cheese or prepare dinner over a *fornello*, once attacking a scorpion with a toothbrush, another time gathering handfuls of cyclamen or wild Christmas roses in the hills.

His first acquaintance in Gargnano was a hunchbacked painter who came with his mother and their maid to live in the upper story of the Villa Igéa. "He talks a bit of weird, glutinous French," Lawrence comments, then more or less goes back to practicing basic Italian with an olive picker: *"Fa bello tempo, oggi."* And soon they were entertaining their first visitor, Signora Samuelli, the German landlady of the

Hotel Cervo, who was *"fearfully* honoured at the thought of coming to afternoon coffee" with "a howling gentleman and swell." Because Signora Samuelli was a "strict housewife" who sometimes called Frieda to account, Lawrence had to spend an afternoon scrubbing the bedroom and cleaning the silver before she came.

And Signorina Feltrelline, their teacher of Italian, with her black gloves and slight squint, was a "screaming farce" and something of a martinet. "I can't help drinking a little wine, to assert my masculine and marital independence," he writes, but "like humble children, F. and I lisp our lessons."

At other times, Frieda complained about the soldiers who insisted on howling all through the night, tipsy on wine, and banging tambourines when the wounded returned from the Tripolitan war. Lawrence thought that the soldiers were "so good looking an animal." The women of the town would sometimes tread the wine grapes in the streets and in their courtyard, and Signor Pietro di Paoli, who may have had his aristocratic, monkeylike visage preserved in the portrait of the "foreign gentleman" in *The Rainbow*, sent them "baskets of figs and grapes and weird fruit." Fourteen years later, Lawrence decided to translate the "little novels" of Giovanni Verga, perhaps because certain scenes recalled this happy period to him.

One feels that the ambience of Lake Garda is caught by the reflected radiance of Lawrence's delight in his new surroundings, and his letters from this period are full of imagery, soft yet sparkling, precise and simultaneously evocative, even in the details of mundane domestic life. Reading these letters, his disciple Henry Miller found himself disgusted by what he calls "Lawrence's workingman's attitude about things" like scrubbing floors, cooking, and laundering. Miller thought that these letters exposed a man demeaning himself in domestic chores.

Chores notwithstanding, Lawrence resumed the rewriting of *Sons and Lovers*. By early November it was finished and in the hands of Edward Garnett. During the process of completing that novel, Lawrence established his characteristic habits of work: like a master gardener sculpting a precious shrub, he rewrote a piece by "pruning it and shaping it and filling it in," until it had become an entirely new creation.

By January of 1913, he was embarked upon a major novel. It was tentatively called "The Sisters":

> I have done 100 pages of a novel. . . . And it is good, too, I think, do you know, I have inside me a sort of answer to the *want* of today: to the real, deep want of the English people, not to just what they fancy they want. And gradually I shall get my hold on them.

Yet by the end of that month, as he was departing from the Villa Igéa, he was so discouraged by the formlessness of the material that he dropped the book after writing two hundred pages in order to take up another novel he was doing more or less with his left hand. Temporarily entitled "The Insurrection of Miss Houghton," it would become *The Lost Girl*, his first novel to use Italian characters and setting.

After a day's work at his desk, Lawrence participated to some degree in the village life around him:

> I go in a little place to drink wine near Bogliaco. It is the living room of the house. The father, sturdy as these Italians are, gets up from the table and bows to me. The family is having supper. He brings me red wine to another table, then sits down again, and the mother ladles soup from the bowl. He has his shirt-sleeves

> rolled up and his shirt collar open. Then he nods
> and 'click-clicks' to the small baby, that the
> mother, young and proud, is feeding with soup
> from a big spoon. The grandfather, white-
> moustached, sits a bit effaced by the father. A
> little girl eats soup. The grandmother by the
> big, open fire sits and quietly scolds another
> little girl.

Writing about the domestic felicity of the Italian peasant, Lawrence is also envisioning his own past: the scenes of his own secure boyhood, the evenings of closeness between himself and his father, the rough-and-tender yet almost mindless communication that bound together the members of his own family before the simple sensuous ways of his father became an intolerable cross laid upon the ambitions of his mother. The feelings aroused by these domestic scenes at Gargnano seem to have found their way into his revision of *Sons and Lovers*.

Beyond the threshold of their dwellings, these peasants seemed to be no less delightful:

> The Italians sing. They are very poor, they buy
> two-penn'orth of butter and a penn'orth of
> cheese. But they are healthy and they lounge
> about in the little square where the boats come
> up and the nets are mended, like kings. And
> they go by the window proudly, and they don't
> hurry or fret. And the women walk straight and
> look calm.

In the vitality, warmth, and pride of the peasants Lawrence sensed a quality of being that was born in an instinctive way of life, and he concludes: "I think they haven't many ideas, but they look well, and they have strong blood."

A little later, he writes to his friend Ernest Collings:

> Instead of chasing the mystery in the fugitive,
> half-lighted things outside us, we ought to look
> at ourselves, and say, 'My God, I am myself!'
> That is why I like to live in Italy. The people are
> so unconscious.

To another friend, he says about the peasants, "They are a spunky lot, and no soul or intellect. It's an awful relief to live among them." Later in "Autobiographical Essay," he describes with similar warmth "the human flow" that came to him from these Italians and the "silent contact" he had with them—which, he adds, saved him from complete isolation into which he was withdrawing as a result of his dissatisfaction with urban society.

Indeed, living among the instinctive Italians threw these dissatisfactions into clear relief. An instinctive individualist with an urge for order, he began to gather his insights about industrialism and Italians into a pattern, a kind of presiding principle of life that was to be shaken from time to time but never shattered. He was now proclaiming his theory of blood consciousness. These ideas he expressed in two places: in *Twilight in Italy* and especially in the famous letter to Ernest Collings:

> My great religion is a belief in the blood, the
> flesh, as being wiser than the intellect. We can
> go wrong in our minds. But what our blood
> feels and believes and says is always true. The
> intellect is only a bit and bridle. Why do I care
> about knowledge. All I want is to answer to my
> blood, direct, without fribbling intervention of
> mind, or moral, or what-not.

The statement is quoted frequently by critics, often derisively. Lawrence himself later seemed to recognize that he had overstated the cause for "blood consciousness."

Bertrand Russell later called his theory "rubbish that led
straight to Auschwitz." Austin Harrison, the successor to
Ford Madox Hueffer as editor of the *English Review,* sees him
as a reactionary, preaching a return to primitive life forms
and idealizing blood sacrifice, and calls his view in general
"inherently close to the fascist conception of society." Lawrence's views are easily misunderstood but what they represent is a private dream rather than a political plan or design,
and it is best to approach them through individual psychol-
ogy and the precise analysis of the moment in Western culture that encouraged their emergence. Bald political terms,
with their inevitable crudity of labeling, provide no illumina-
tion in this particular context. For all the coincidence of one
or two preconceptions, neither Mussolini nor Hitler could
find any use for Lawrence in their cultural propaganda, and
he certainly could not have found any use for their ideas.

Placed against the background of the period just before
the outbreak of World War I, when people like Lawrence
"saw only too clearly the machine guns hidden behind the
altar-cloth of established religion," with the European mind
at the end of its tether, Lawrence's faith in the peasant personality and his belief in their instinctual behavior seems far
less dangerous and idiosyncratic to us than to many of his
contemporaries. Lawrence foresaw the significance of the
then new theories of Freud, which he learned about through
Frieda and an Austrian doctor who had been Freud's pupil.

Frieda remembers that Lawrence's belief in the blood was
a "living experience" with him, not something that he read
about in a book or heard from her—an experience that
"made him love, not hate." Indeed, the sense of hot discovery in his writing of this period and the contribution of
each discovery in the unfolding of the idea suggests that
Lawrence derived his conviction not from a book by Freud or
from a conversation with friends (though he read omnivor-
ously and talked endlessly), but through the acts and obser-

vations of living itself, as it were through his skin. Lawrence did not "receive" ideas; he felt things directly as experience, as process.

Thus, the theory of "blood knowledge" emerges as Lawrence's response to the problem of man as it posed itself at the time: man is a stranger to himself and must discover or rediscover who he is and what his meaning is. Kierkegaard had sought out the religious center of the Self, which meant a radical return to the Christianity of Christ, not of organized Christendom and its Churches. Lawrence recommended a rediscovery of something even more remote and primitive: of the primitives who existed by their senses before civilization had blighted man's instincts. The Christ whom Lawrence discovered in the Tyrolean crucifixes projected this primitive quality of being, and some of it had been preserved—though now threatened by the Machine—in isolated pockets of people such as the Bavarian and Italian peasants. This same spirit had flickered in Lawrence's father (Morel) and as if to prove that the senses of the father are visited upon the son, had burst into expression in *Look! We Have Come Through!* Most of the Italian poems in this section are hymns to the humanity of the blood.

Interpreted in this way, Lawrence's belief in the blood may be related to a tradition of thought that stems from the Greek worship of Dionysius, the god of drunken ecstasy who made the vine revive in the spring and brought all men together in the joy of intoxication. It flows gently beneath the teachings of Christ, follows the banks of theology in Kierkegaard, merges with a social current in Tolstoy, and receives a most eloquent formulation in Nietzsche, but basically it is the same stream of belief: we live not by the head, but by the heart, not by what we acquire, but by what we are given. It is, in reality, a concept of Grace.

But the comparison should not be pursued beyond a point, for Lawrence never developed a sense of sacrifice to anything but his art ("One has to be so terribly religious to be an artist"). He writes in a letter:

> The real way of living is to answer to one's wants. Not 'I want to light up with my intelligence as many things as possible' but 'For the living of my full flame—I want that liberty, I want that woman, I want that pound of peaches, I want to go to sleep, I want to go to the pub and have a good time, I want to look beastly swell today, I want to kiss that girl, I want to insult that man.'

This letter, reminiscent of passages in "The Spinner and the Monks" (*Twilight in Italy*), sharpens and expands an idea that passes through the mind of Siegfried, the protagonist of *The Trespasser,* just before he decides to commit suicide: "To have no want, no desire—that is death." As he watched the peasants of Gargnano responding directly to their daily desires, Lawrence came to connect the expression of desire with a fundamental approach to existence: the acting out of the deepest impulses was part of the pagan way of life, "the old affirmation of immortality through procreation, as opposed to the Christian affirmation of immortality through self-death and social love." The denial of this pagan spirit— Lawrence often uses the Nietzschean term "Dionysian" as a synonym for it—is equivalent to "self-death and social love": the denial is a will to "death in the flesh," a kind of ego paralysis that had characterized the civilization of northern Europe, and now, in the wake of industrialism, was threatening to descend upon Italy itself, one of the last surviving strongholds of the affirmative impulse in life.

We should note here a development that provides a key to Lawrence's fiction and perhaps explains better than anything else the intensity of his revulsion for England at this time and the reciprocal intensity of his affection for Italy. In

Twilight in Italy, Lawrence links the encroachments of industrialism with "self-death" and the denial of desire: in both instances, man submits himself to something outside of himself, be it a social principle or a means of earning a wage, that his nature does not want. Here Lawrence appears to be fumbling toward a theory that would relate to one another two of man's most basic drives—his sexual and social, to show how the frustration of desire could work underground and emerge in horrid and unsuspected symptoms.

Dionysius reborn might become a savior-god for the human race, everywhere encrusted with time and caste. In *Sons and Lovers*, Mrs. Morel's aspirations for Paul born of a class distinction no longer valid lead him toward a "death in the flesh." While revising this novel, Lawrence realized how dangerously un-Dionysian her direction was, but he simply could not fit these insights into the book without rewriting it entirely.

However, in a short story written or revised at Lake Garda, "Her Turn," this pagan spirit insinuates itself upon the English scene in the brief but disturbing appearance of Frederick Pinnock's daughter. The proprietress of the Golden Horn, where Radford spends his evenings, is puzzled by this wild-looking girl and asks him whether he thinks she would make a good wife for his son. Radford observes that she would be unsuitable for the delicate Willy because she puts her own desires before everything else, "she would only see what she wanted—" But this quality of selfishness (if selfishness it be) is an expression of approval, not disapproval, for later the girl is described by Radford as "full of life" and by the voice of the narrator as a fine swarthy animal, a flash of the Pan. That there is no conflict between Radford and the narrator is made clear in a letter from Lawrence to Ernest Collings: folk like Radford are "so nice"—the precise phrase he uses to describe the Italian peasants to his sister.

Clearly the moral climate of Italy ("it leaves the soul so free") quickened Lawrence's distaste for the north European sense of sin and its dry passion for duty. Both were part of what he called "the Not-Self." "The Not-Self" seems to be his version of Nietzsche's "will to power," a will that expressed itself through the longing for domination or for martyrdom. One was the high road to power, the other the low road, but both led to the negation of Self, which for Lawrence was no road, but merely "the joy we have in being ourselves." In a review of Georgian poetry which he wrote at Garda, he states: "I worship Christ . . . but I do not worship hands nailed and running with blood upon a cross. . . ." This polarity seems to have its parallel not only in the title, but also in the duality of images in "The Spinner and the Monks." The image of the Dove suggests the warm blood, the dark and hidden below, while the image of the Eagle is associated with the imperious, commanding will to power. Later, in Mexico, the idea represented by the image of the Eagle was to absorb the meaning of the Dove idea, but at this time it stood for the impersonal, dispassionate will that serves something other than the Dionysian spirit.

Chapter 2

THOUGH Lawrence told friends early in 1913 that he loved Italy and would continue to live there for "a bit," the world, the weather, and other things were intruding upon his idyllic isolation. The days were turning unbearably hot for an Englishman accustomed to the Midlands climate. Frieda, missing her children and wanting to see them again soon, would lie on the floor in misery and then get "fearfully angry" with Lawrence because he refused to urge her to stay for his sake. Frieda's divorce had been promised for that summer and Lawrence wanted to be married in England as soon as it was granted. Funds were low and Lawrence had to find means of bringing in money with more regularity than the advances and small royalties that his writing promised.

There was another source of discord. "L. always wants to treat women like the chicken we had the other day, take its guts out and pluck its feathers, sitting over a pail," Frieda writes in her *Memoirs*. Once, while they were washing up, he told her that women had no souls and could not love. Frieda broke a plate over his head and ran away for two days.

And despite the best will in the world, Lawrence felt like an outsider in paradise. This feeling is conveyed in "The Spinner and the Monks."

Describing a little old woman spinning flax on a terrace of San Tommaso, he indicates the gulf that separates the sophistication and self-consciousness of the northern European from the eternal, self-centered wisdom of the Italian peasant: "In her universe I was a stranger, a foreign *signore*. . . . She had cut off her consciousness from me. So I turned and ran away, taking the steps two at a time, to get away from her." Similar alienation is expressed in his letters: "We had six months without anybody at all. One needs some people to keep healthy and well aired," he writes to one friend, and a short time later, to another: "We are tired of being buried alive."

The last two essays in *Twilight* (which describes his walking tours in Switzerland and his meeting with Italians in exile) suggest that Lawrence was determined to carry on his quest elsewhere for whatever it was he was seeking— perhaps a place where the spirit and the senses could be unified in harmonious flow, where the integration of the personality was possible, where he would meet, in words from *Look! We Have Come Through!*, "this unknown that I would trespass on." Lawrence headed for the Mediterranean, convinced that industrialization was crossing the Alps into northern Italy.

Before starting for the south, he and Frieda decided to spend "two or three days" of the Easter vacation at San Gaudenzio, a mountain resort about three miles away, then to tour Italy via Verona, Florence, and Rome, where Frieda's sister Else was to reserve a *pensione* for them. This "mountain retreat," in reality little more than a six-room farmhouse operating illegally as an inn in the evenings, was run by a peasant family named Capelli for whom Lawrence developed great affection (in *Twilight*, he describes them as typical of the peasants' strengths and weaknesses, changing their name to Fiori possibly to protect the identity of a son who planned to escape conscription). Furthermore, a friend of the Garnetts, a "Mrs. Anthony" who had visited the couple at Villa Igéa, was staying at San Gaudenzio alone and apparently the mutual need for communication played a part in their plans.

At the end of March, he and Frieda bade their Gargnano friends good-bye, packed their suitcases, closed up the Villa Igéa, and went donkey back to San Gaudenzio. Five days later, Lawrence wrote to David Garnett:

> It is a lovely place. There is a garden over a mile round, with vines and olives. It falls to the cliff edge above the lake. . . . The mountains are covered with snow opposite.

To his sister Ada he added these impressions:

> We love the people of the farm, such warm folks—at evening we play games in the kitchen. On Sunday there was a band of 4—cello, *mandolino*, and 2 guitars playing in a corner queer lovely Italian music while we danced. The peasants of the mountain were in. One was a good looking wild fellow with a wooden leg. He danced like anything with Frieda. . . .

Lawrence was never to be in better physical and psychological health than he was during April of 1913, though Frieda added an unhappy postscript to this letter. ". . . L. had made me so miserable that I began to think I was scum of the earth, unfit for a human being—*His* misery was *all* my doing." The joy and enthusiasm he expresses in these letters apparently reflected his mood more truly than the implications of Frieda's somber note, born in part out of insecurity about the future, in part out of guilt over her enforced separation from her children, and in part out of the normal frictions of living together.

Thus, when Frieda's wish to visit her children without any

detours caused Lawrence to cancel their Roman holiday, it
was easy to let the "two or three days" drift into two weeks.
The joyous, lightning sketches of that fortnight (to David
Garnett and to his sister Ada) suggest that he had already
regretted his decision to leave; on the other hand, the
four essays about San Gaudenzio—"San Gaudenzio," "The
Dance," "Il Duro," and "John"—which he wrote later in
order to fill out the contents of *Twilight*, continue the mood
of ambivalence expressed in the first three essays.

This period is also described in Tony Cyriax's *Among Italian
Peasants*, but the book has almost nothing to add to Lawrence's far more enjoyable accounts of quiet evenings with the
five Fioris, of the wild dancing into the night, of the hikes
into the unspoiled countryside, of the young men emigrating to America. Tony Cyriax was the "Mrs. Anthony" of the
letters, an artist who was hiding from her husband, a crazed
Swedish painter (it may be worth noting briefly that Alvina
in *The Lost Girl* leaves England shortly after the maddened
Dr. Mitchell makes threatening advances to her). Mrs.
Cyriax further distinguished herself by dubbing Lawrence
"Lorenzo." (It will be of interest to collectors of nicknames
that Lawrence was also known to Italians as "Signore Lav-
renchy," "Meester Low-RENTS," and *"le scrittore Inglese."*)

During these two weeks, he apparently resumed work on
the novel he had started at Gargnano. To Edward Garnett,
he writes:

> I sit and write in a deserted lemon-garden
> which gathers the sun and keeps it . . . . I did 200
> pages of a novel—a novel I love—then I put it
> aside to do a pot-boiler—it was too improper.
> The pot-boiler is at page 110, and has developed
> into an earnest and painful work—God help it
> and me.

The first reference is to a novel conceived at about the same time that the manuscript of *Sons and Lovers* had been dispatched to his publisher. Lawrence had intended to take a rest between works, but in the middle of December of 1912, he had come down with a cold that confined him to bed in Gargnano. To pass the time, he planned a new novel—"a sort of life of Robert Burns." He adds, "But I'm not Scotch. So I shall just transplant him to home—or to the hills of Derbyshire—and do as I like with him as far as circumstances go, but I shall stick to the man." In a letter written on Christmas Eve, he had told Ernest Collings that he was "writing a bit at a new novel" and as relaxation, copying prints by Peter de Wint and Frank Brangwyn, the English painter. A few days later, he writes: "I've stewed up my next novel inside me for a week or so, and have begun dishing it up. It's going to have a bit of a plot, and I don't think it'll be unwieldly, because it'll be further off from me and won't come down on my head so often."

The fragment of an unfinished novel, presumably the one about Burns, appears in Edward Nehls's composite biography of Lawrence, but it seems to have no connection with Burns. Either this novel was discontinued or given a new direction. It seems likely that Burns, the farmer-poet, took shape as Tom Brangwyn, the farmer "full of heavy blood" who loved poetry but hated print, whose farm was located near Derbyshire. When Lawrence got deep into this novel provisionally entitled "The Sisters," he decided to divide it into two, the first a study of husbands and wives, the second of men and their mistresses. But this was to come, and by the time he left Italy he had just about finished the first draft—it would undergo seven revisions before attaining its final form in 1915.

Before returning to England, Lawrence and Frieda visited Verona for a few days and there, as planned, met Frieda's sister, Else Jaffe, who was coming up from Rome. Else had played the Good Samaritan the year before by putting them onto Alfred Weber's apartment in Icking. Shortly before Lawrence and Frieda left Italy, she came to their rescue again by offering them the Jaffe summer cottage at Irschenhausen while her husband was teaching in Munich. In Verona the details of the occupancy were arranged (Else was second only to Edward Garnett as the most loyal friend Lawrence had during those first precarious years with Frieda; he paid his respects to both by dedicating *Sons and Lovers* to Garnett and *The Rainbow* to Else).

On April 14, Lawrence and Frieda left the Hotel Europa e Aquila Nera and took the night train through the Brenner Pass out of Italy. The memory of this experience is recorded again in a brief scene toward the end of *Women in Love*, when Ursula announces to Birkin that she wants to leave the frozen world of the mountaintops:

> "Well," he said, "we can go away—we can go tomorrow. We'll go tomorrow to Verona, and find Romeo and Juliet, and sit in the amphitheatre [presumably the Arena which is the largest in the Roman world after the Coliseum]—shall we?" "Yes," she said softly, filled with relief. She felt her soul had new wings, now he was so uncaring. "I shall love to be Romeo and Juliet," she said. "My love!"

Ursula and Birkin point south, but Lawrence and Frieda headed in the opposite direction. Three days after leaving Verona, the couple was installed in the Jaffes' "jolly little wooden house . . . standing in a corner of a fir-wood, in a hilly meadow all primulas and gentian and looking away at the snowy Alps."

The creative impetus that Lawrence had generated in the surroundings of Lake Garda seems to have spilled over into the two months he spent at Irschenhausen. Frieda fears that he has become a "writing machine" and Lawrence accuses himself of turning out "bloody rot," but the activity of this short period is impressive: he pushed the first drafts of "The Sisters" and "The Insurrection of Miss Houghton" several stages closer to completion; wrote at least three short stories including the one he regarded as his best up to that time, "The Prussian Officer"*; drafted the lines for eight of the poems in *Look! We Have Come Through!* and finished several that were to appear in *New Poems*. To Garnett he writes, "I am only doing review for the *Blue Monthly*," and mentions a "biography" that he wrote and sent off with the review of *Sons and Lovers* to Mitchell Kennerley, who published the American edition. In May, his short story "The Soiled Rose" (later "The Shades of Spring") was printed by John Middleton Murry's publication, *The Blue Review* (formerly *Rhythm*).

Though Lawrence worked productively at Irschenhausen, a lovely spot not far from the place where he and Frieda had passed their "honeymoon" the previous spring, he was not content. While praising the beauty of Bavaria to his sister Ada, he is simultaneously bemoaning to Edward Garnett the boredom it induces:

> I *have* suffered from the tightness, the domesticity of Germany. It is our domesticity which leads to our conformity, which chokes us. The very agricultural landscape here, and the distinct paths, stifles me. The very oxen are dull and featureless . . .

Even the Bavarian peasants whom he had apotheosized in *Twilight in Italy* had suddenly lost their charm: ". . . the folk seem like tables of figures . . . . Over these countries, Ger-

---

*Despite his German name, the orderly resembled an Italian peasant in appearance and temperament; on another level, he represented the spirit of the Dove opposed to that of the Eagle.

many and England, like the grey skies, lies the gloom of the
dark moral judgment and condemnation and reservation of
the people."

Throughout his stay at Irschenhausen he longed for what
he had left. Less than a week after leaving Italy, he writes to
Garnett: "I wanted to go back to Italy . . . . I have longed for
Italy again, I can tell you." And to A. W. McLeod, a friend
and fellow teacher in Croydon, "It broke my heart to leave
Italy. I still cannot believe that this landscape is real. I expect
it to lift and clear away, and reveal my bright Garda again."
To Helen Corke he confides a month later: "I may come to
England for a short time. I don't want to. I want to go back to
Italy."

And in reporting his English itinerary to Garnett, he
states:

> We might stop a week at the seaside. One gets
> to long for a touch of salt in the air. Then we
> move to Italy again—probably, for a time at
> least, to San Gaudenzio. I hope that I shall be
> able to have enough money for all this.

This was how the future wobbled when Lawrence and Frieda arrived in England on or about June 21, 1913, for a visit
that lasted some seven weeks. Most of this time was divided
between the Cearne, Edward Garnett's summer house in
Kent, and an apartment they rented on the sea at nearby
Kingsgate ("the place *bores* me . . . We bathe and I write
among the babies of the foreshore"). At the end of July, they
went up to London for a few days; from there Frieda
departed for Metz to visit her parents before they took the
waters at Baden-Baden, while Lawrence returned to Kingsgate and later attended the wedding of his younger sister
Ada to Edward Clarke in Eastwood. During these seven
weeks, Lawrence and Frieda made some friends who were to

be important throughout Lawrence's career: Edward Marsh, the editor of *Georgian Poetry*, John Middleton Murry and Katherine Mansfield (whom they met in the editorial office of *The Blue Review* in Chancery Lane), and the Asquiths (especially Lady Cynthia).

On August 8, Lawrence left England, and three days later was reunited with Frieda at Irschenhausen. His second stay (five weeks) at the Jaffe cottage was happier but less productive than the first. Though he complains about the incessant rain that "positively stands up on end" and the constant flow of visitors, he is relieved to be out of England. Returning to his roots had touched nothing vital in him, nor provided sharp contact with anything: "Everything seems to have been ravelled and dull and woolly." On the other hand, Munich was *"so frei und lebendig"*: there were the mountains that "go up and down across the sky," the evenings of beer-drinking by lamplight, and the Sunday excursions to the *Markt* in Wolfratshausen.

In early September of 1913 he writes to Garnett: "It is beautiful here, but one feels transitory. . . . I shall not be able to settle down here to work, I know." Despite this pessimism, Lawrence was able to pursue a new version of "The Sisters" so energetically ("I am working myself blind") that he had hopes of finishing it by October. Between bouts with this book, he wrote a number of lines of verse, some of which probably coalesced at Cornwall into " 'And oh—that the man I am might cease to be—'" and "Mutilation" in *Look! We Have Come Through!* He also did one sketch on Eastwood (unidentified but possibly the "Adolf" published in 1920 by the *Dial*) and two on San Gaudenzio which, along with the sketches that Austin Harrison was about to print in the *English Review*, would become part of *Twilight in Italy*. He began to receive some money for the numerous pieces appearing in various publications. He continued to work on "The Sisters," but the "earnest pot-boiler" which he mentions in the previously cited letter to Garnett had become so "fearfully exciting" to him that it temporarily displaced the novel "meant to be for the *'jeunes filles.'* " In April, 1914, he writes again to Garnett:

> I can only write what I feel pretty strongly about: and that, at present, is the relation between men and women. After all, it is *the* problem of today, the establishment of a new relation, or the readjustment of the old one, between men and women.

In context, this remark seems to apply to the "earnest" and "fearfully exciting" pot-boiler (*The Lost Girl*, then provisionally known as "The Insurrection of Miss Houghton"), but somewhere in the concurrent composition of the two novels, the burden of that theme transferred itself to the second part of the "sisters" novel (later *Women in Love*). In the exhaustive yet intensive process of exploring the relationship between Ursula and Birkin and Gudrun and Gerald, Lawrence probably drained the dramatic power out of the theme.

Irschenhausen, as before, made Lawrence dream of Italy. In his first letter from Germany on August 11, he speaks wistfully of spending the winter under the warm sun of the Italian Riviera, near Lerici: "There will be the Mediterranean, and the mountains, and my beloved Italy." A week later, he writes to Lady Cynthia Asquith: "We are going to Italy in a month or so. Then we think of Lerici, somewhere near Leghorn—Shelley and Byron tradition. It might be good for my rhythms" (Edward Marsh said that Lawrence wrote poetry in "rag-time").

Early in September, their plans became firm and called for Frieda to visit her parents again at Baden-Baden while Lawrence, with rucksack on his back and "The Sisters" in the rucksack, walked through Switzerland to meet Frieda in Basle. From Basle, they would go together to Lerici (as it turned out, Frieda extended her stay at Baden-Baden and joined him in Milan instead of Basle). On about September 16, Lawrence left Irschenhausen for Überlingen, where he took a steamer that carried him across the Boden Sea to Constance. He spent the day exploring that medieval city with a curiously un-Teutonic flavor ("I love these old towns with roofs sticking up so high, and tiles of all colours—sometimes peacock and blue and green"), and on the following morning, went down the Rhine on a small steamer to Schaffhausen. That afternoon he crossed the Swiss border and spent that evening at the Inn of the Golden Stag in a "village of tall, quaint houses flickering its lights on the deep-flowing river."

The following day he walked through "mile after mile of dead, uninspired country" until he came to Zurich, a city which he found to be, despite its picturesqueness, "soul-killing." After a brief rest and a Swiss meal, he again boarded a steamer which left him about three-quarters of the way down the Lake of Zurich. He "climbed a long hill from the lake, came to the crest, looked down the darkness of the valley, and descended into the deep gloom, down into a soulless village," where he took accommodations for the evening (at the Gasthaus Zur Post). There he encountered the Italian workers whose activities, along with this leg of his journey, provided him with the substance of "Italians in Exile," the penultimate chapter of *Twilight in Italy*. That evening, Lawrence won their confidence by telling them about his intention of walking down to Italy and living there again; later on, when they had retired to a nearby café which was a "warm, ruddy bit of Italy within the cold darkness of Switzerland," they in turn told him about their unrequited nostalgia for the sun of Italy, their refusal to return, and their dreams of a better future for the working man. Giuseppino, their leader

who made such a deep impression on Lawrence, gave him a
copy of a little anarchist paper published in Geneva. Many of
the opinions that he expressed were to be voiced later by
Parkin, the Marxist gamekeeper in the first version of *Lady
Chatterley*. Indeed in appearance as well, the Italian exile of
"pale clarity and beauty" is reminiscent of the celebrated
gamekeeper.

But perhaps the most memorable experience happened at
the Gasthaus, when Lawrence was permitted to look on
while his "new" Italians rehearsed an amateur melodrama
for an approaching carnival. As he watched these simple folk
throw themselves into their roles under the direction of
Giuseppino, no doubt Lawrence felt himself returned to the
mood of the theatrical performances at Gargnano, recounted with delightfully amusing details in the chapter of
Twilight in Italy called "Theatre." But he senses that something more than the mere pleasure of playacting animated
these exiles: at work was a powerful guiding spirit absent
from the more polished performances of the professional
troupe that enacted D'Annunzio, Ibsen, and Shakespeare at
Garda. This spirit was the spirit of Giuseppino:

> In him was a steady flame, burning, burning,
> burning, a flame of the mind, of the spirit,
> something new and clear, something that held
> even the soft, sensuous Alfredo in submission . . .

The flame of this free spirit in Giuseppino informs the
rehearsal with its magic quality that touches the common-
place with beauty:

> It was strange to watch them on the stage . . .
> moving subject round Giuseppino, who was
> always quiet, always ready, always impersonal.
> There was a look of purpose, almost of devotion
> on his face. . . . The . . . men seemed all overcast,

mitigated, in part transfigured by the will of the little leader.

The following day he resumed his journey, the remainder of which is narrated in "The Return Journey," the final chapter of *Twilight*: "So on I went," he writes, "by the side of the steamy, reedy lake, walking the length of it. Then suddenly I went in to a little villa by the water for tea." There, attracted by the two elderly sisters and the "delicate" dog who kept the place, Lawrence lingered for a while, pretending to be an Austrian from Graz. But this was carrying the "people's theatre" too far, and fearing to be unfrocked as an impersonator, he "went on to a detestable brutal inn in the town." The next day he reached Lucerne and its lake, but like the Zurich scene, it was irritating to him—"like the wrapper round milk chocolate"—and therefore he "took the steamer down the lake, to the very last station and there found a good German inn." At this inn he met an Englishman who reminded him of how different his own people were from the Italians, who dramatized the difference between acting out of desire and acting out of will.

The next day he embarked upon the long climb up to St. Gotthard Pass. Lawrence liked the villages because they had the "atmosphere of being forgotten, left out of the world," but the mountains were an ominous metaphor to him, a concept that becomes part of the fabric of *Women in Love.* Descending the southern slope of the Alps toward Airolo in Italian Switzerland, his mystical soul felt restored: "It is as if the god Pan really had his home among these sun-bleached stones and tough, sun-dark trees. And one knows it all in one's blood, it is pure, sun-dried memory." In Airolo, he talked Italian and felt himself back in Italy again (Italian is the language of the canton of Ticino). A train carried him the dozen miles to the "great, raw high-road" through the Ticino valley to Bellinzona, and as he walked down this new

great road, "desolating, more desolating than all the ruins in
the world," his blood rebelled and his spirit sank. This valley,
with its quarries, railroads, and smoking factories was "sort
of a nightmare" reminiscent of the English industrial towns.
The sight of the Italian laborers working all day, "engaged in
the mere brute labor . . . shockingly indifferent to their
circumstances, merely callous to the dirt and foulness," saddened and terrified him. This was the fate of the peasant
who left his home and became a workman. These corrupted
Italian peasants had lost all connection to his beloved folk of
Gargnano: the "disintegrative process" of mechanization
creeping across the Alps on the new Italian highway was
spreading a new quality of sordidness into the Italian soul.

     After spending one night in Bellinzona and another in
Lugano (". . . here in this holiday-place, was the quick of the
disintegration, the dry-rot, in this dry, friable flux of people"), he crossed into Italy itself at "dreary little Chiasso,"
took a streetcar over to the Lake of Como ("it must have
been wonderful when the Romans came there. Now it is all
villas") and then a steamer to the city of Como, where he
spent the night in a "vast old stone cavern of an inn, a
remarkable place, with rather nice people."

     At Lake Como, Lawrence decided that he should take a
train for the last fifty kilometers of the trip. Something
about the terrible nervous energy of "beastly Milano, with
its imitation hedgehog of a cathedral, and its hateful town
Italians" both elated and depressed him on a very deep level
of consciousness, but these impressions were to wait nearly
ten years before they emerged in *Aaron's Rod*. Drinking a
Campari in the Cathedral Square on a bustling Saturday
afternoon, he waited for Frieda and watched northern Italy
in the process of change.

     When Lawrence changed his destination from Lake Garda
to Lerici, he was also concluding that the future of the
senses lay farther to the south. Under the Mediterranean

sun, away from the smoke of factories, perhaps a measure of paradise could be regained. While leaving Milan with Frieda on the train headed for the Riviera di Levante, his senses may have been assailed by the vision that visits Ursula when she finds herself, at the end of *Women in Love*, in a parallel situation:

> Now suddenly, as by a miracle she remembered that way beyond, below her, lay the dark fruit-ful earth, that towards the south, there were stretches of land dark with orange trees and cypresses, grey with olives, that ilex trees lifted wonderful plumy tufts in shadow against a blue sky.

Lawrence and Frieda must have reached La Spezia, a pleasant port on the Riviera di Levante which used to be the home of the Italian navy, on September 28 or 29 and may have stopped to call on Thomas Dacre Dunlop, the British consul whose wife was later to type the final draft of *The Rainbow*. Since his letters make no mention of doing so, it is likely that they did not stay overnight in La Spezia, but caught the steamer service across the Gulf of Spezia to Lerici ("a beautiful ride in a dirty steamer for 40 minutes"). In Lerici, they stayed for about a week at the Albergo delle Palme, "a delicious hotel—6 francs a day pension, jolly good food, wine and all included—a big bedroom with a balcony just over the sea, very beautiful."

Now there is a huge mural testifying to the rich literary associations of the area. Depicted in various poses are Dante, Shelley, Byron, Trelawny, Wagner, and Lawrence. Under the impression of Lawrence gazing wistfully across the superb crescent of the gulf is the legend: "*Perche non ritorna, Cristo fra questi ulivi?*" ("Why does Christ not return to us, among these olives?") The hotel now has a pillbox in front of it, a memento of World War II. Five minutes by foot

at San Terenzo is the house where Shelley dwelt before he
met his death, and a few miles to the south at Viareggio,
where his body was washed up, is the home where Ouïda,
second only to Lawrence as a writer of Italian impressions,
spent her last days in obscurity.

Almost immediately Lawrence found a *villino*, a "four
roomed pink cottage among vine gardens" about three miles
from Lerici by foot and less than a mile by water, at a spot
called Fiascherino. Located on a "little tiny bay half-shut in
by rocks, and smothered by olive woods" that sloped down
to the sea, it could be reached only through a gate on the
beach that opened onto a path of stepping-stones up to the
house or through a narrow footpath that wound its way up
from Lerici through the stone pines hanging over the sea.
The nearest village in this wild country was Tellaro, a picturesque fisherman's village perched on a rock, which the
sea smites and sucks. The place suited Lawrence's purse as
well as his preference for isolation—the rental was eighty-
five lire a month for everything, including the furnishings
and the servants. As soon as the proprietor, Ettore Gam-
brosier, had finished harvesting the crops on the property,
Lawrence put Frieda, his suitcases, and himself in a rowboat,
and after steering a shaky course across the inlet, took possession of the *villino*.

Chapter 3

LAWRENCE describes this interlude as "a dream." Subtropical nature produced a kind of Wordsworthian tranquillity and expansion of spirit in him, and while supping in the grape arbor called the "Belvedere" or writing on the *palazzina* that descended in terraces to the sea, he would listen to the robins and finches as they sang among the red leaves of the vine or watch the lizards whip about on the rocks or merely admire the wild narcissus and yellow crocus that twinkled in the sunshine not far from the sweet violet and purplish crimson anemones. He had the English country boy's fondness for domestic animals and he announces with elation that his favorite black hen has returned from its wandering and complains in mock horror that Mino the cat, who likes to sit on his knee, will give him fleas. Mino appears in Chapter 13 of *Women in Love* called "Mino," as Birkin's frisky young pet who disciplines a stray cat. Ursula insists that he is a "bully like all males," but Birkin defends him as a model of "male dignity" and of "higher understanding."

The sea provided Lawrence with other simple pastimes. He discovered the comfort and fulfillment of rowing his own boat (and often the discomfort when the seas turned "muscular"). He fished with the peasants and with an admixture of admiration and aversion, describes the local technique for catching cuttle fish.

> Alessandro caught inkpots: and like this. He
> tied up a female by a string in a cave—the string
> going through a convenient hole in the end.
> There she lived, like an Amphitrite's wire-
> haired terrier tied up, till Allesandro went a-
> fishing. Then he towed her, like a poodle
> behind. And thus, like a poodly-bitch, she
> attracted hangers-on in the briny sea. And
> these poor polyp inamorati were the victims.

He found unexpected pleasures after dark in watching the
"lighthouse beating time to the stars" or in bathing by
moonlight:

> The full moon shines on the sea which moves
> about all glittering among the black rocks. I go
> down and bathe and enjoy myself. You never
> saw such clear, buoyant water. Also, I don't
> swim more than a dozen yards, so am always
> trying to follow the starry Shelley and sit amid
> the waves.

Often he sat peacefully on the rocks and watched the
fishing boats and strange sails that "like Corsican ships come
out of nowhere," or read while the olives shimmered and the
figs burst in the wonderfully fertile atmosphere of the sun
and the sea. It was as though time had been turned back.

The cobbled path through the olive woods into Tellaro set
him to dreaming of the past. To Will Hopkin, an Eastwood
friend in whose home Lawrence had met many prominent
Socialists of the day, he writes:

> I am always expecting when I go to Tellaro for
> the letters, to meet Jesus gossiping with his dis-
> ciples as he goes along above the sea, under the
> grey, light trees. . . .

This scene provided the setting for the short novel *The Man Who Died*.

Occasional trips to La Spezia, sometimes with pages of "The Wedding Ring" (as the first half of "The Sisters," later *The Rainbow*, was then called) for Mrs. Dunlop to type, or perhaps on a trip to bring back a piano for Frieda, allowed him to view this scene from another angle:

> I am writing on the steamer, going to Spezia. It is a wonderful morning, with a great, level, massive blue sea, and strange sails far out, deep in a pearl glow, and San Terenzo all glittering pink on the shore. It is so beautiful, it almost hurts. . . .

And toward the end of this same letter to Henry Savage, the English biographer and essayist whom he had met in Kent in 1913, he says:

> The mountains of Carrara are white, of a soft white blue edelweiss, in a faint pearl haze—all snowy [the marble cuts create the illusion of snow]. The sun is very warm, and the sea glitters.

From the mountains themselves, the scene was spectacular:

> Yesterday we climbed the hills above the sea . . . and we saw the sea coast curve in a fine, fine line far away into the heavens, with towns like handfulls of shells, Massa, Viareggio, and ships like butterflies in mid-air.

Lawrence's language remains fresh and free of clichés, his prose conveying the rhythm and mood that he associates with the scene he is describing. Few writers can produce the "penumbra of place" better than Lawrence, and few places inspired him to do so as did the Italian scene.

As at Lake Garda, the exotic surroundings stirred in him a yearning for domesticity: he made his own wine and bottled twenty-five liters of it, picked and preserved figs, helped Frieda to make pumpkin jam, browsed in the Tellaro shops for vegetables, and with his braces tied around his waist, scrubbed the floors of the *villino* Bijou (so he named it) until Elide, his servant, exclaimed in admiration, "*Ah, l'aira e la pulizia*" ("Ah, air and cleanliness"), and he himself sang, "Lord, to see the dark floors flushing crimson, the dawn of deep red bricks rise from out this night of filth was enough to make one burst forth into hymns and psalms."

There were few household luxuries for Frieda, but she apparently was happy with an open fireplace over which she could cook pasta and fish, a piano which had been transported by steamer, rowboat, and Italian back, two servants, and a man whose muse visited him even in their narrow kitchen.

About the house, next to performing domestic duties himself, Lawrence enjoyed nothing better than watching his servants do them. He found the older Felice irresistible:

> She is a rum creature—about sixty, and wizened, and barefoot. She goes barefoot, walks with half a hundred-weight of charcoal on her head, like a queen wearing a crown, and whistles her acquiescence when you ask her to do anything. She is a jewel . . . very funny and ceremonious. When Elide has put the soup on the table, she says '*Arrivederci*, eh?' before she can leave us.

Felice's family name was Fiori. Lawrence, it will be recalled, changed the name of the Capelli family at San Gaudenzio to Fiori when he wrote *Twilight in Italy*, so that Maria

Capelli, who "had been a housekeeper, a servant in Venice and Verona before her marriage," becomes the Maria Fiori immortalized in this family portrait. This blending of names suggests that part of Felice Fiori may have gone into the picture of Maria Fiori and that the composite portrait may be a crystallization of what Lawrence considered to be the salient features and characteristics of both the southern and northern peasant women.

During this period, Lawrence fell in and out of love (mainly in) with the Italian peasants all over again. He spent days picking olives, singing, and chattering with them, language difficulties apparently no great barrier. On one occasion, while eating with the owners of the Bijou, he observes that they "fling all their scraps and 'bouts de vin' on the floor unceremoniously, and the cats and flies do the war dance about them." He visits the *contadini laggiu* ("the peasants down yonder"), "awfully nice people" who occupied the only other house on the bay, and they strike him as so congenial that he thinks about keeping the cottage for the following winter. Felice's cousins sometimes come and play the guitar and invite Lawrence and Frieda to sing with them. "It is jolly. Liugi is very beautiful—and Gentile is a wild joy. How happy you would be with these people," he tells Will Hopkin. He wrote to May Holbrook, sister of Jessie Chambers (Miriam of *Sons and Lovers*): "We have heaps of friends here. This morning early came a little priest from the Seminary at Sarzana, to bring us a little music: the school-mistress from Tellaro will come this afternoon to tell us of her love affair with Liugi." On Christmas Eve, a group of peasants call on the couple, and at midnight, they all sing the *Pastorella* together.

At Tellaro, on Sundays, Lawrence enjoys the performance of the agile *saltimbanchi* [acrobats] in the open air, and during the week looks on as the local fishermen spear octopus ("You never saw anything so fiendishly ugly") for the *padelli* of the natives, or indulges his newly acquired taste for snails. "In patent leather boots and black suit, playing *Signore*," he attends the wedding of a young peasant couple and participates with great gusto in the *pranzo* [the meal] and "high jinks" that follow the ceremony. At one point, he is so enchanted with these simple folk and their ways that he writes, "If I had a son, I wonder what I should call him — something exciting like Severino or Benedetto."

Lawrence took deep pleasure from these pastimes, else he would not have bothered to record his impressions in such vivid detail. Throughout he sounds happy and healthy, even though he was constantly beset by financial anxieties. Yet his frail physique made him prone to fatigue and easy exasperation. Richard Aldington observed that there was something within Lawrence, that antithetical "dark self," which led him to do and say disconcerting and inconsistent things. Lawrence's moods fluctuated with the weather and his health, and though he could express the happy ones in language that lends his letters a unique quality, he could also give vent to his vituperation and his moments of disenchantment with a frankness that seemed to at least one person "a fantastic lack of restraint." At about the same time that he is telling one friend that the "Laocoon writhing and shrieking" have gone from his writing, he writes to another: "If you but knew the thunderstorms of tragedy that have played over my wretched head, as if I was set upon on God's earth for a lightning conductor, you'd say, 'Thank God I'm not as that poor man.' . . . We are the most unfortunate, agonized, fate-harassed mortals since Orestes and that gang."

Sometimes he is in the dumps: "God, how weary I am of women, women, eternal women. Do you know, there are here, in Lerici at present, seven mortal English women, and I the only man under fifty-five. And a man of fifty-five to me is more or less of a matron. Dear heaven, I should like to join the army, or go into a monastery." Occasionally he broods about the Italians. When, with typical Mediterranean indifference to efficiency, the bank at Spezia neglects his instructions or the picture framer fails to finish a job on time, Lawrence curses them "right and left" and confides to Edward Marsh, "I hate them and want to stamp on them." When the pianoforte man at first refused to transport the instrument via rowboat, he again rages: "I loathe and detest the Italians. They never argue, they just get hold of a parrot phrase, shove up their shoulders and put their heads on one side, and flap their hands."

Lawrence needed the stimulus of black brooding in the more or less imaginary dumps; he chafed over the lack of respectability and Frieda still brooded over the separation from her children; and both at times were concerned about their financial plight. The need to be English came at him with a rush at such times as the afternoon spent with the popular Russian novelist Amfiteatrov and his family, whose exotic and alien ways hit him squarely and brought back a sense of his roots.

If such memories and mishaps vexed Lawrence to nightmare, then events of a more formidable nature saddened the sympathetic observer in him. Italian men were emigrating in droves from the nearby villages to America, and as in the north of Italy, peasant life in the south was disintegrating and a feverish life of activity was replacing the old slow rhythms and stability. The beauty of sun and sea could not balance the inequities of an outmoded system, and the plight of common clay moved him to a compassion that is partly commiseration (financially, the second Italian sojourn was one of constant worry for Lawrence). The men, he writes to May Chambers Holbrook, will no longer stay in Italy without money:

> They work and slave, they make a living, and
> save a little. But in ten years of America they

> can save as much as in a hundred years
> of Italy. . . . Italy is a country on the change, and
> suffering acutely. Fifty years ago, almost every
> man was a peasant. In one generation it has all
> changed.

But like the occasional thunderclouds that obscured the sun of La Spezia, these black moods vanished quickly. They were not fed by loneliness and isolation, as at Lake Garda. There, he had been entirely dependent upon the natives for social community, and the more subtle kind of communication necessary to every articulate person was not available to his rude Italian. But at Lerici their social life was different. They were received cordially, even feted by their fellow expatriates at Lerici, until Frieda later insisted on telling everyone the unvarnished truth about their state of sinfulness.

But they maintained several of their associations right to the end of their stay. Lawrence speaks about lunching at the Pearses, "who have a beautiful house where the Empress Frederick [sic] of Germany spent a winter with them." At Christmas, they took dinner with some neighbors named Cochrane and attended services in their private chapel ("lambs we looked, I can tell you"). They got on well with the chaplain, a Reverend John Wood, "hired by the wealthy and impossible Cochranes, who fling gold at the Italians around and bruise their faces." Through friends at Aulla, they met a family named Huntingdon. Mrs. Huntingdon, who had read *Sons and Lovers* without being shocked, disapproved of the liaison, but behaved with kindness and consideration.

Perhaps their most fruitful friendship was with Thomas Dacre Dunlop. Dunlop and his wife played host to the couple on several weekends, but more important, she typed one of the drafts of *The Rainbow*, the book that Lawrence was finally finishing. Later, after Dunlop was moved to a post in the East, Lawrence may have acknowledged his indebtedness to the diplomat by inserting him very briefly into "The Lovely Lady" as the father of Pauline Attenborough: "her father had been a consul in the East and in Naples: and a devoted collector of beautiful and exotic things."

Despite the limited facilities of the Bijou, Lawrence repeatedly extended hospitality to his friends in other places. Edward Garnett, John Middleton Murry, Katherine Mansfield, Henry Savage, W. H. Davies, and the Hopkins were unable to accept, but in January of 1914, Edward Marsh and James Strachey Barnes (later to become a vociferous admirer of Mussolini) arrived at Lerici. Lawrence met their boat, and as the three of them struggled up the slope laden with luggage, they were roundly cheered by the delighted peasantry, who mistook them for traveling acrobats. In the spring of that year, they entertained Herbert Trench, a poet of repute and distinguished if solemn personality who was living in Florence. Trench told them about the glories of Florence and also explained the secret of the origin of life—it had to do with a mystical doctrine of spirals.

There were other visitors who reminded them of "home." Constance Davidovna Garnett, the wife of Edward Garnett, and the translator of Dostoevski, called upon the couple and probably whetted Lawrence's appetite for the Russian novelist. Ivy Low, the young writer who later married Commissar Maksim Litvinov, undertook a worshipful pilgrimage to the feet of the "genius" who had, in her opinion (shared by Rebecca West and Viola Meynell) composed three novels "unrivalled, in depth and insight and beauty of language, by any other contemporary writer." Lawrence must have invited her to come (the letters have disappeared), for she borrowed passage money and Catherine Carswell's best clothes to see him. She left, bewildered and shaken, after a stay of six weeks, during which Lawrence's critical eye found out all her defects, "one by one, and quite a few that no one else discovered." Frieda may have participated in the sniping, for later, Compton Mackenzie was pained by the way "Frieda was forever encouraging her Lorenzo with boisterous laughter to pull people to pieces."

Either Ivy Low or Mrs. Garnett introduced the Lawrences to the small Russian colony and Amfiteatrov. It was a "rum show," Lawrence wrote of the Amfiteatrov household. "Twenty-six people at lunch, a babble of German, English, Russian, French, Italian" and a house full of "scuffling servants and cultured children." Here Lawrence met the adopted son of Maxim Gorki, who had lived on Capri, and his "great wild Cossack wife," and one wonders whether he met the then unknown Boris Pasternak, who was touring in that area before returning to Russia. Though all this commotion made Lawrence feel "very English and stable and stolid in comparison," he loved these Russians "for their absolute carelessness about everything but just what interested them."

But perhaps the most memorable encounter of that period occurred in the midst of the peasant wedding where the wine was "running very red." Lawrence, who had been playing *Signore* in patent leather boots and black suit, was summoned from the festivities to greet three Georgian poets who had come unexpectedly to call. They were Lascelles Abercrombie, Robert Trevelyan, and Wilfrid Wilson Gibson. They were accompanied by Mrs. Abercrombie and a stranger named Waterfield, who had, on the request of Edward Marsh, brought the poets from Aulla to see the rising young novelist and poet. Apparently the transition from a wedding feast of octopus, chicken, vino, and "crude, strong, rather passionate men" to Anglo-Saxon bards proved too sudden for Lawrence: the rarified atmosphere of his "vague countrymen" made him feel so top-heavy that he staggered and lost his bearings.* He ran here and there to

---

*Mrs. Lascelles Abercrombie ("she awfully jolly, and a fine true-metal sort that I love") apparently noted nothing amiss in Lawrence's behavior. In "Memories of a Poet's Wife," *The Listener*, November 15, 1956, she wrote: ". . . we certainly walked the last part of the way along the shore until we

make his guests comfortable before returning to the feast of fish and fowl. "A table full of chickens," he said to Waterfield, "with their legs wild in the air, you know how they look." Waterfield took an instant liking to this gaunt, consumptive-looking writer and invited him to visit his Fortezza at Aulla.

Lawrence accepted the invitation, and one spring afternoon he and Frieda arrived at the castle for a weekend stay. Mrs. Waterfield was startled by the sight of Frieda dressed in Bavarian national costume which showed her buxom figure to full advantage, but it was the "lithe, frail-looking young man with the alert blue eyes and whimsical smile" who attracted her. Lawrence seemed to like the Waterfields, and during lunch, he learned that Aubrey Waterfield was a young English painter who had been drawn to Italy in search of the right woman as well as the right conditions for his canvases. The young woman was Lina Duff-Gordon, who had lived in a villa near Florence with her aunt, the formidable Janet Ross. Miss Gordon had grown up in the company of such notables as Bernard Berenson, Bertrand Russell, and John Addington Symonds. She had married Waterfield and soon afterward the couple had leased a sixteenth-century fortress from one Monty Brown, an Englishman who liked to collect Italian castles. They had settled down in the Fortress to live the simple bucolic life and to entertain infrequent guests such as the Baroness Orczy, Lord Stanhope, Robert Trevelyan, and Lawrence.

---

came to Fiascherino, when great shoutings and screamings arose, and over the sea from round a rocky point came a small rowing boat with a large piano balanced most precariously on it—one man rowing with an oar from the stern while another man hung on to the piano, screaming with terror. Then out of a cottage dashed Lawrence, and with other men landed the piano and bore it away in triumph. Lawrence then saw us, and greeted us charmingly, explaining that there was a wedding on, and the reception was to be held in his cottage—so we all joined in and drank healths to the happy pair."

During the conversations after lunch, the subject turned to his now famous *Sons and Lovers*. Lawrence asked Lina Waterfield, herself a writer, what she thought of the book. Mrs. Waterfield answered that Paul's mercy killing of his mother did not seem consistent with his professed love for her and struck a "false note." Lawrence answered emphatically: "You are quite wrong. You see, I did it—I gave the over-dose of morphia [to my mother] and set her free." Mrs. Waterfield was stunned and bewildered by the confession and Aubrey Waterfield was led to remark, "With his charm he is very egotistical and unbalanced."

Lawrence seemed to enjoy the remainder of his visit and the castle surprised him: "he darted into every corner, ran down each tower and looked at the view from every angle. His keen interest in everything was infectious." When he saw Aubrey Waterfield's frescoes on the walls of the dining room, he gave "little squeaks of delight" and wanted to do some painting himself. Lawrence's own letters suggest some ambivalence about the castle, but no doubt he liked the company of the Waterfields.

One day in the spring Lawrence invited them to Fiascherino and cooked them a great dinner by himself. He amused them with his stories about the cinema people who had come to his promontory to film *Ulysses and the Sirens* and about how the men with flaxen wigs had to impersonate the Sirens because the Italian girls refused to face the camera. The Lawrences returned to Aulla for another long weekend.

Shortly before leaving Fiascherino, Lawrence came on short visits alone. During these visits, Mrs. Waterfield must have described the attractions of life in nearby Florence and recounted her childhood memories of John Addington Symonds, the author of *History of the Renaissance in Italy*, a collection of essays which was widely read during Lawrence's youth for their prose poetry and word portraits. Lawrence must have enjoyed hearing her recollections of Symonds, for in the previous year he had published a story called "The Shades of Spring." The protagonist, John

Adderly Syson, resembles in nature as well as in name that English expatriate whose impressionistic reflections about Italy left their mark upon the style of Lawrence's *Twilight*.

On one occasion at the castle, Lawrence met a chemist from the dynamite plant at Villafranca, a man named Soddy, who had brought along the local apothecary, Dottore Iorio. The *dottore* sang in a *mezza voce* that shook the stones of the Fortress (however, it still stands, albeit in disrepair, now a government property about to become a national monument) and Soddy caught Lawrence in a corner and made him listen to his adventures in Mexico, where he had lived for years. The idea of a man with a Mexican background who lives in Italy and who narrates a story, Ancient Mariner style, to an English listener may have provided Lawrence with the nucleus of a story he was to write ten years later, "None of That!"

The Waterfields had to leave their fortress when Monty Brown decided to renovate it for more affluent Englishmen, but Lina Waterfield's impressions of Lawrence in her *Castle in Italy* help to fill out our picture of the poet among the peasants. Often she merely strengthens an impression we may gather from his letters: "He had a real understanding and liking for the Italian people, especially the peasants and the workers. They often irritated him, but their friendliness and lust for life overshadowed their faults in his eyes." Despite his grousing ("I wish we were not with so many people here, I want to feel free"), he impressed the Waterfields by the warmth with which he responded to the various types of people he met through them in the Lunigiana. Lawrence continued to correspond with the Waterfields for a time after they reached England, and according to Lina Waterfield's granddaughter, Mrs. Jocelyn Lubbock, there were many valuable letters from Lawrence to the Waterfields and to their daughter Kinta (now Mrs. Jack Beevor) which were destroyed during World War II. Though Lawrence and Frieda soon were to follow the Waterfields, the four were not to meet again until fourteen years later in Florence.

By early June, the weather along the Riviera di Ponente becomes uncomfortably hot for people accustomed to northern climate. Furthermore, Frieda wanted to see her children, Lawrence wanted some summer travel, and uppermost, both of them wished to be married in England now that Frieda's divorce had finally been granted. Mrs. Huntingdon took them over to the lighthouse island of Tino for a farewell picnic. The Pearses and the Cochranes gave them a final dinner and both of them felt "queer and loose at the roots, in the prospect of leaving our Fiascherino." A letter to Waterfield suggests that Lawrence was rather vague and slightly despondent about their imminent departure:

> We leave here either in the beginning or middle of June. My wife wants to spend three months in England. But I don't know if we shall be there so long. I would rather be in Bavaria or the Black Forest than in England. We have an invitation for the Abruzzi [from the Baronessa di Rescis] and to Florence for the first three weeks of October [from Frederick Herbert Trench].

Lawrence and Frieda planned to depart from Genoa by ship and then to stay in London at the South Kensington flat of Gordon Campbell, the Irish barrister who would one day as Lord Glenavy be the director of the Bank of England; then while Frieda was staying with her parents in Baden-Baden, Lawrence would divide his time among the Garnetts, the Abercrombies, and Gibson. In August, he would join Frieda and together they would meander back to Lerici by late October with stopovers in Abruzzi and Florence.

However, "because of filthy weather," the first stage of the itinerary was canceled, and instead of going to Genoa, Frieda took off by train for Germany and Lawrence on foot for Switzerland and France. At La Spezia, he was met by an engineer named Lewis from the Vickers-Maxim works. The dates of his correspondence show that the first leg of the

journey must have been a train ride to Turin. On the tenth
of June, the hikers were in Aosta, and by the evening of the
twelfth, they had reached the St. Bernard Pass, resting at
the hospice (which is still free to overnight guests) "in a
lovely little panelled room." After a week in Switzerland,
they swung west into France. By the last week in June, the
incredible walking tour was completed and on June 27, Lawrence was having lunch with Edward Marsh, Frieda, and
Rupert Brooke at the Moulin d'Or in Holland Park, London.
Unfortunately for readers who find the account of his earlier walking tour among the gems of travel literature, all
that grew out of this trip were calluses on Lawrence's feet.

Two weeks after Lawrence and Frieda were officially
declared man and wife, World War I broke out. Five and a
half years were to elapse before he would set foot on Italian
soil again. Afflicted by the restlessness of spirit and the poverty of means that the returned prodigal must often endure,
increasingly despondent over the course of the war, Lawrence moved from place to place (frequently provided by
hospitable friends) where he could work.

More than five years as a reluctant repatriate provided
Lawrence with the conditions which may have been essential to the development of his art. He was restrained from
extensive travel that could expend his fluctuating store of
energy; in turn, this confinement, however unwelcome ("I
shall go mad, because there is nowhere to go"), established a
stability lacking in his life as an expatriate. Thus, with this
respite from movement, he could guide a number of works
through the final stages of publication; and furthermore, he
could at leisure and from a distance evaluate and distill his
Italian experience.

PART II

Return to Italy

(November 1919–February 1922)

Chapter 4

THOUGH Lawrence's novels kept his name before the reading public, they brought him very little money. He had to borrow and to struggle along on the charity and kindness of friends and family in order to survive. The English winter was straining his health and he was already "sick to death" over the war. The English establishment, which forced him into bankruptcy court because he would not pay Frieda's divorce costs, was causing him to dream about abominable beetles. Whatever hope they may have held of living in England on the modest if significant support his work was receiving was quenched by *The Rainbow* affair followed by the "spying" episode in Cornwall.

In November of 1914, while they were living in Buckinghamshire (Chesham), the stories that he had either conceived, written, or polished at Gargnano had been published by Duckworth under the title imposed by Garnett against Lawrence's will, *The Prussian Officer and Other Stories*. This volume added luster to his growing reputation and created interest in the other work that he was preparing for the press. Just about a year later (in September of 1915) Lawrence delivered a masterpiece to his countrymen, *The Rainbow*. Reviewers descended upon it, hip and thigh. Their howls of Victorian indignation alerted "the censor-morons" (the term was coined by Lawrence) to the polluting presence of an "orgy of sexiness," even before the book got onto the bookstore shelves. A thousand copies were seized by Scotland Yard, acting upon the Obscene Publications Act of 1857 as misinterpreted by a "constipated booby who should have been publicly purged" (Compton Mackenzie). Finally, an "elderly ass of a magistrate," Sir John Dickinson, ordered all copies of *The Rainbow* to be destroyed. The publisher of the book, Methuen, put up no resistance. Martin Secker offered to take on the suppressed novel in order to secure the rights to *Women in Love,* but he warned that no bookseller would at that time buy a single copy of *The Rainbow* even with a reputable imprint on it unless he sold it as curiosa. Needless to say, this brutal act was a severe blow to a writer pressed for money, in poor health, and in low spirits, and the English reader who wanted to enjoy this highly moral book had to import it from America or wait fourteen years for its republication.

The real reason behind the charges of alleged obscenity, Richard Aldington believed, was that Lawrence had denounced the war. Gilbert Cannan, a novelist friend, also blamed the suppression of the book on war hysteria.

Not long afterward, the Lawrences were hounded out of Cornwall by the same kind of hysteria. The natives of Zennor suspected them of cooperating with German submarines off the coast, and the police ransacked their cottage when they were accused of deliberately violating blackout As a result, they were ordered to leave the area within three days, to stay out of "prohibited areas," and to report to the police whenever they moved. In *Not I, But the Wind,* Frieda says, "When we were turned out of Cornwall, something in Lawrence changed forever."

Distrustful now of the "democratic process," Lawrence knew he had to leave England,* and for a while considered

---

*In light of the insults Lawrence was forced to endure, admittedly in a country at war, it is hard to appreciate Emile Delavenay's characterization of Lawrence's response to this treatment as "the spoilt child whimperings of a Lawrence vainly hoping to escape from a sinking Europe to go and 'sell his stuff' in America." *The D. H. Lawrence Review 8,* no. 1 (Spring 1975): 86.

sailing to Spain or Palestine or going to Russia (*"nuova speranza—la Russie"*) where the peasants had just overthrown the czars. But these plans were unrealistic and perhaps passing fancies. Yet he was determined to go, and in his more practical moments, he fully expected to return to Italy— presumably to Fiascherino, where beloved old Felice Fiori was minding some of the small possessions and manuscripts that he had left behind. So sure was he that he would soon be off that he invited Amy Lowell to "come and see us soon" at the Lerici cottage (which he hoped to reoccupy). And to Koteliansky, the translator of Chekhov, he writes, "I must go to Italy again." The coast of Cornwall reminded him of Tellaro, and to Lady Ottoline Morrell, we find him confiding: "I would like to be remote, in Italy, writing my soul's words."

Those words might have been taking shape already around an incident that had scandalized the entire countryside: while Lawrence was there, a neighbor in Cornwall had horrified her aristocratic family by marrying her cowman, some years her junior. The drama of this romance percolated in his imagination until he was ready to create a novel around it almost ten years later. In preparation for his day of departure, Lawrence brushed up on his Italian by reading Michelangelo, Matilda Serao, Grazia Deledda, Verga's *Cavalleria Rusticana,* Manzoni's *I Promessi Sposi,* and a great deal of D'Annunzio.

But a dark age was advancing upon Europe, even upon Italy itself, and Lawrence began to dream of establishing a new order in an uncorrupted place where it would be eventually possible to know "a good peace & a good silence & a freedom to love & to create a new life."

This dream was enthusiastically supported by a young clerk working in the Russian Law Office, whom Lawrence had met on a walking tour of the Lake District (Lewis, the Vickers engineer from La Spezia, was also along). Lawrence christened the utopian colony "Rananim," a word derived from a Hebrew song that Koteliansky used to sing to him. He thought that twenty carefully chosen colonists would be the optimum number and he wanted John Middleton Murry, Mark Gertler, the painter, "Kot" Koteliansky, and Katherine Mansfield to be among its founders. At first he thought it might be located on the "forsaken estate" in Florida that had been offered to him by the English composer, Frederick Delius, and then considered Garsington estate, with Otto-line Morrell as the "queen of the colony." Katherine Mans-field threw cold water on the idea, Garsington proved to be "very bad, really," and Delius, no utopian himself, withdrew the offer when he discovered Lawrence's intentions. Law-rence was to travel all over the world on his quest, but at the time he thought it possible that America, the promised land for so many generations of Europeans, might furnish the site of the ideal community. He had been immersing himself in the literature of America and felt prepared to engage the "new consciousness" which he felt was emerging there. His work was being well received by Americans and America even held the promise of freedom from financial anxiety.

Lawrence was prepared to sail for the "new unknown" when British authorities refused to renew the passports they had been granted two years earlier (possibly because of Lawrence's outspoken opposition to the war and because Baron Manfred von Richthofen, the German war ace, was a distant cousin of Frieda's). Before Lawrence could protest the decision, America had declared war on Germany, and the die was cast. "America is a stink-pot. . . . [it] sends ice to my heart" he grates to his friends through his disillusionment. Although he encouraged the publisher, Ben Heubsch, to arrange an American lecture tour, for the time being the dream had been shattered and his bitter denunciation over America's "perfidy" carried over into his virulent digressions on American tourists in "Fenimore Cooper's White Novels" (*Studies in Classic American Literature*). How else can we account for the irrelevancy and indignation of those passages in which Americans are depicted as vandals advancing upon the Bargello, the Piazza di San Marco, and the other "beautiful things of Europe"? Indeed, he concludes in waspish exasperation, "the golden cupolas of St. Mark's in Venice are turnips upside down in a stale stew, after enough American tourists have looked at them . . . Poor Europe!"

And so by the fall of 1919, "poor Europe" once more pulled at the Lawrences—albeit from different directions. Frieda was eager to see Germany again, and Lawrence, wearied by the war, by the climate, and at times even by his wife, longed for the warm waters and peaceful, ancient parapets of Italy. Fond as he was of the old baroness mother, "he shrank just then from visiting Germany. He would go later." Frieda would join him in the north of Italy and together they would head for the soothing sun, to house themselves among the peasants for at least the winter. Earlier, he had reluctantly changed his mind about living at Fiascherino. "It is always lacerating," he had written to Mrs. Thomas Dunlop at La Spezia, "to go back to the past: and then to find our beloved old Felice more old, and unhappy for death of poor Elide— no, couldn't stand it."

In October, when their passports were finally granted, Frieda left for Baden, and Lawrence prepared to depart for Italy. He asked Catherine Carswell, the Scottish novelist who had written a favorable review of *The Rainbow*, if she could help him find a "very simple room in Rome" through her cousin Ellesina Santoro, who lived there, and announced, "I am going to Caserta, near Naples—hear of a farm there." His informant was Rosalind Popham, who had been married to Dr. Godwin Baynes when Lawrence first knew her in Berks, and the farm was a small place at Picinisco belonging to the family of Orazio Cervi, who had served as an artist's model in London for Rosalind Popham's father, the sculptor Sir Hamo Thornycroft.

About November 10, he came down to London for final farewells, and early on the morning of the twelfth, he took the train at Charing Cross. Only the Carswells and Kotelian-sky were present to see "the solitary pilgrim" off, and as a part-ing gift, the Carswells gave him a black-and-white shepherd's plaid (the one that figures in *Sea and Sardinia*). Gladdened though his heart was by this gesture, his mood as he departed from England a second time is no doubt mirrored in the lonely passion of his hero in *Kangaroo*:

> . . . England, England which he had loved so bitterly, bitterly, and now was leaving, alone, and with a feeling of expressionlessness in his soul. It was a cold day. There was snow on the Downs like a shroud. And as he looked back from the boat, when they had left Folkstone behind and only England was there, England looked like a grey, dreary-grey coffin sinking in the sea behind, with her dead grey cliffs and the white worn-out cloth of snow above.*

To conserve the small legacy left to him by Rupert Brooke, Lawrence crossed Europe without the benefit of a berth. The sit-up journey in a crowded coach turned out to be tedious: "The train sits still half the time to hatch out her ideas for the next kilometre." He paused briefly in postwar Paris ("a nasty city"), then continued through the Alps to Turin. There he called upon Sir Walter Becker, a wealthy English shipowner known throughout Italy. The Beckers offered him the hospitality of their villa, and Lawrence, short on funds, accepted. In a letter to Cynthia Asquith, the only one that describes his journey south, Lawrence sum-marizes his weekend stay in a crisp paragraph, dwelling

---

*Yet Lawrence could also write in 1922 from Italy: ". . . we made a mistake forsaking England and moving out into the periphery of life . . . . we're rather like Jonahs running away from the place we belong . . ."

entirely on the "sincere, half-mocking argument" he had with the "important old wolf," Becker arguing for "security and bank-balance, and power," Lawrence for "naked liberty." They ended up hating each other—"with respect." Lawrence was to transform this brief encounter into one of the central episodes of *Aaron's Rod.* His other impressions of this interlude he expanded skillfully if maliciously into Chapters 12, 13, and 14 of the novel, changing the scene from Turin to Novara (which he was not to visit until 1920) and the Beckers into the Franks. Sir Walter later took exception to the portrait of himself as "dull."

At this juncture, Lawrence and Aaron took different routes. Lawrence rode the train straight down to Genoa, then continued along the coast "beside a lovely sunset sea" (*"bello, bello, il mare!"* he cries out in a letter) to La Spezia, where he stayed with the Dunlops. Aaron, on the other hand, moves east to Bologna (after being chauffered to the train in a limousine), then Milan where he registers at the Hotel Britannia, "because it is not expensive, and English people went there." Aaron is given "a little room with a tiny balcony, looking on to a quiet street . . . a home of his own once more." Later, he falls into the "restless, nervous drift of the north Italian crowd" on national holiday, visits the cathedral (the largest Gothic structure in Italy) with its "numerous spires pricking into the afternoon air," and later is shocked by a violent political demonstration which, like the one later in the novel, makes the Fascist movement seem imminent. Though this chapter catches the depressed mood of the city, Lawrence's vivid impressions of the cathedral and his fresh feeling for the energy of "beastly Milan" both seem to belong to an earlier experience (before World War I had started) when he walked across northern Italy on his way to Fiascherino.

Aaron in the novel heads directly for Florence in the company of two English painters, but Lawrence, before swing-

ing down to Tuscany, first stopped at Lerici (again at the
Albergo delle Palme) and visited old friends. This was the
beginning of Italy for him, the real Italy, and he writes to
Cynthia Asquith:

> The sea is marvellous—yesterday a blazing, blaz-
> ing sun, a lapping Mediterranean—*belleza!* The
> south! The south! The south! Let me go
> south . . .
>   Italy is still gay—does all her weeping in the
> press—takes her politics with her wine, and en-
> joys them. Great excitement over the elec-
> tions—but lively and amused excitement—noth-
> ing—tragic or serious.

At first Lerici made Lawrence lyrical, but his reactions on
his return were typically mixed and dependent upon the
weather. The second day at Lerici was gray and angry and
induced more somber reflections in a lonely Lawrence:

> It is evening and the lights twinkle across the
> harbour, and the lighthouse beats time with the
> same measure as six years ago: yet everything
> seems different—not so gay any more.

Lawrence was beginning to fret at Frieda's absence, and
clearly he was looking forward to reestablishing their inti-
macy amid the surroundings of romantic Florence. Even if
Norman Douglas had not been able to secure an apartment
for them as he hoped, the time had come to move on.

On the following day, under lowering skies, Lawrence left
Lerici for nearby Sarzana to catch the afternoon train for
Florence. He pulled into the station of Santa Maria Nouvella
during a dreary drizzle, "buttoned up in my old thick over-
coat, and with my beard bushy and raggy because of my

horror of entering a strange barber's shop." Depositing his bags at the luggage check, he walked (to save cab fare) to Thomas Cook's on the Via Tornabuoni for messages and found awaiting him "a kind and practical note" from Douglas directing him to a *pensione* near the Piazza Mentana, where he himself was living. On his way down the Lungarno, "watching the first lights of evening and the last light of day on the swollen river," Lawrence found Florence unlike the joyous, sunny city he remembered from the prewar days: it "seemed grim and dark and rather awful in the cold November evening." Near the Ponte Vecchio, his glum reflections were interrupted by a familiar voice:

> Isn't that Lawrence? Why of course it is, of course it is, beard and all! Well, how are you, eh? You got my note? Well now, my dear boy, you just go on . . . straight ahead, straight ahead—you've got the number. There's a room for you there. We shall be there in half an hour. Oh, let me introduce you to M——.

It was Douglas, prepared to befriend Lawrence as he had before in England. Douglas was living in a *pensione* on the Lungarno delle Grazie, near the Piazza Mentana. In the same house lived Pino Orioli, the owner of a bookshop and Douglas's inseparable companion whose flair in publishing had ensured a competence for his friend and in the future would serve Lawrence well. Douglas, according to D. M. Low, was an impressive figure, tall, and with an easy bearing indicative of great strength, always carefully dressed, a good malacca crooked over his arm, alert and debonair. He had a formidable face which would yet swiftly relax into jovial greeting. The author of *South Wind* had in tow a naturalized American named Maurice Magnus, who claimed to be an illegitimate grandson of Kaiser Wilhelm. An aspiring author himself, he had just finished his "memoirs" of the French Foreign Legion (in which he claimed to have served) and wanted to meet the young Englishman whose reputation had preceded him. This meeting was to develop into a sporadic and strange relationship between the two exiles.

Douglas and Magnus trotted off to the post office and Lawrence by himself hunted up the Pensione Balestri at 5 Piazza Mentana, not far from the Cavelotti area and there "waited in an awful plush and gilt drawing-room and was given at last a cup of weird muddy-brown slush called tea and a bit of weird brown mush called jam on some bits of bread." Finally he was taken up to his chamber on the third floor of the big, ancient Florentine house. There was a "big and lonely, stone-comfortless room looking on to the river." With only nine pounds in his pocket and twelve more in reserve, Lawrence was happy to have this inexpensive room (ten lire a day) which Douglas, who had wanted Lawrence in an adjoining room on the second floor, described with a contemptuous snort as "Spitsbergen!" But Lawrence must have felt like Aaron in Chapter 16 of *Aaron's Rod:*

> He rather liked the far-off remoteness in the big old Florentine house: he did not mind the peculiar dark, uncosy dreariness . . . He preferred the Italian way of no fires, no heating. If the day was cold, he was willing to be cold too. If it was dark, he was willing to be dark. The cosy brightness of a real home—it had stifled him till he felt his lungs would burst. The horrors of real domesticity. No, the Italian brutal way was better.

From the open window of his room, he could watch, "as if he were in a castle with the drawbridge drawn up," the bonneted mules and the umbrellaed carters crossing the

Arno "swollen with heavy rain," and the dogs of Florence performing their doggy functions on its yellow banks, the latter a sight that never failed to enrage him. He could also watch the young *Vandervogels* from Germany exploring the city of their recent foe. Despite such diversions, Lawrence in his letters sounds lonely and a trifle depressed over the changes that Italy had undergone in five years. He writes to Catherine Carswell: "Am here in the rain, waiting for Frieda, of whom I hear nothing yet [en route to Germany, she had lost her trunks in Holland, and had run into a "nightmare of a muddle," of harassments, and delays because she was German]. Italy is rather spoiled by the war—a different temper—not so nice a humour by far." It is possible that Lawrence may have been referring to an unfortunate incident, "not so nice," up at Fiesole. While climbing on a crowded train, he had his wallet stolen. When he discovered the loss of his cash, he felt first "the sensation of as if his beard dropped through the soles of his feet, then the mounting fury that flushed him to the roots of his hair." The experience left him disillusioned with his fellowman, including the Florentine: "One gets into a silly soft way of trusting one's fellows. One *must not* trust them, for they are not trustworthy. One must live as the wild animals live, always wary . . ." Lawrence recalled this incident while writing *Aaron's Rod* (Aaron is also robbed), and this mood of *noli me tangere* dominates the concluding chapters of that strange, bristling book.

Lawrence was not inclined to brood over such losses. Though he took them hard, he could shrug them off, according to Catherine Carswell, with "enviable lightness." Furthermore, there was little opportunity to moan over this adversity, for Douglas lost almost no time in presenting the newcomer to his friends, especially Reggie Turner, inveterate inventor of bons mots, loyal companion to Oscar Wilde, and unsuccessful author of twelve novels, twice the number

Lawrence had written. Turner, who lived nearby in a "large airy flat" on the Viale Milton, received a note from Douglas, saying,

> I have D. H. Lawrence with me just now. Would you care to meet him? If so, let me know and I will arrange a quiet dinner somewhere, ONLY WE THREE.
>
> I am going to try to prevent his meeting certain other people, because he is a so damned observant fellow and might be so amused at certain aspects of Florentine life as to use it for "copy" in some book. . . . Read his *Twilight in Italy*. . . . that gives you the key to his nature which is sympathetic and yet strangely removed.

Flapping his eyelids "like a demented owl" (so Lawrence would describe him in *Aaron's Rod*), Reggie invited Lawrence to his apartment. Douglas introduced him to the English colony in Florence. From then on, Lawrence was received by his compatriots with almost none of their typical reserve. In Pasakowski's café or in the other trattoria on the Via Tournabuoni, where the English congregated, he ate, drank, and talked with a circle of new acquaintances that included (beside Douglas and Turner) Magnus, the novelist, Ada Leverson, the Sitwells, Bernard Berenson, Harold Acton, and Percy Lubbock. At other times, like Aaron, he explored the "wet, wet world" of "noisy Florence," listening to the "great, soft trembling of the cathedral bell," admiring the Palazzo Vecchio with its "slim tower that soared dark and hawk-like, crested high above," standing before the "great naked David, white and stripped in the wet, white against the warm-dark cliff of the building," soaking up the sights of the city and searching for the inexpensive gifts (he bought Magnus a bowl of Volterra marble for his birthday) like any tourist. In the evenings, there was whiskey and conversation with Douglas and Magnus, followed by dinner washed down by litres of *vino rosso*. In his introduction to Magnus's *Memoirs of the Foreign Legion*, Lawrence describes those "noisy and unabashed occasions" at the Pensione Balestri (which has been remodeled into a hotel), with Douglas screaming wildly at the waiter in broken Italian that his *zuppa* had "a piece of dish clout in it" and tubby Magnus laughing in his squeaky fashion, his "pink, fattish face" turning yellow. There is no hint in his correspondence that he was storing up the impressions that were to become those vitriolic visions of *Aaron's Rod* or that the fears of Douglas were justified. Instead, in his letters he speaks of his sunny room over the Arno (when the downpours ceased), the good wine, the easygoing *padrone* of the Balestri, and a life of such "nice carelessness" that he felt he could "loaf away his substance."

At four o'clock in the morning of December 3, Frieda arrived in Florence, "a bit thinner for her vegetarianism, but very well," bringing with her their small reserve of money. Lawrence promptly took her for a drive through the city in an open carriage. In the morning haze, they saw the entrancing bridges and the fretted towers of Florence and watched the rays of the rising sun bathe "the great naked man in the dark, strong, inviolable Piazza della Signoria." There, in "one of the world's living centres," both of them must have felt, like Aaron Sisson, a "sense of having arrived—of having reached a perfect centre of the human world." However, Florence had not yet recovered from the "contamination of the war," and the tension Lawrence felt between "perfection" and "contamination" perhaps accounts for the apparently contradictory moods of *Aaron's Rod*, set chiefly in Florence of the postwar period.

The sunny mood transcendent, the Lawrences explored the treasures of Florence and the bare beauty of the Tuscan

countryside before heading south a week later on December
9 for the brief Roman holiday they had planned. In Rome,
Frieda's passport provoked an unpleasant scene. At the *pensione* Ellesina Santoro had recommended, the proprietor
refused to honor their reservations when he discovered that
Frieda was German. Ellesina put them up in her own apartment and almost immediately someone robbed them. Fearing that his hostess would insist on reimbursing them,
Lawrence kept the incident a secret. But as in Florence, this
incident cast a pall, this one enduring, over the short visit.
Next to the "genuine culture" of Florence, Rome seemed
"tawdry and so *crowded* . . . vile." Probably Richard Somers in
Kangaroo speaks Lawrence's mind when he says: "Never
again, he felt, did he want to look at . . . Rome with all the
pressure on the hills. Horrible, inert, man-moulded weight.
Heavy as death." With the exception of the galleries of the
Vatican, which he visited in the company of a young South
African painter whom he had met at the Santoros' (Jan Juta),
little about the freezing city caught his fancy.

On the December 16, the Lawrences were due
to go into the mountains south of Rome, to the farmhouse
of Orazio Cervi, in Picinisco in the province of Frosino. They
planned to stay there for some months, perhaps until early
spring, and then on their way over to Naples, Lawrence, on
the invitation of Magnus who claimed to have an in with the
guestmaster, Don Bernardo, there, was to stop at the great
abbey of Monte Cassino for a few days.

On December 16, the Lawrences started out for Picinisco,
little suspecting that it was in a most remote and "stagger-
ingly primitive" corner of Italy, ringed in winter by mountains that glittered "white like devils." After reaching the
village—then as now a tiny cluster of farmsteads made of
native stone, they had "to cross a great stony river bed [the
Rapido, a major battleground of World War II], then an icy
river on a plank, then climb unfootable paths while a man

struggles behind you with your luggage," in order to reach the Cervi dwelling two miles above town. The house of Cervi no longer stands, the victim of an Allied bomb-blast, but Lawrence's description of it preserves its memory:

> In Picinisco we got right into the wilds, where the ass lived in the doorstep and strolled through the hall, and the cock came to crow on the bent-iron washstand: quite a big, fine-looking house, but lo and behold, one great room was a wine-press, another a corn and oil chamber, and as you went upstairs, half the upstairs was open, a beautiful barn full of maize-cobs, very yellow and warm-looking. The kitchen, a vaulted cave, had never been cleaned since the house was built.

They had to cook their own meals over a wood fire, which had to be blown up in the smoke-blackened fireplace with a long, ancient iron tube that had one foot standing in the ashes. Then, sharing the single teaspoon and plate (one saucer, two cups, and glasses completed the complement of crockery) they had to eat off their knees, all the while blowing up the blaze for warmth. The peasants were fascinating to watch—Lawrence had quit trying to learn their "unintelligible dialect"—the brigandlike men went around in skin sandals and white-swathed strapped legs, women in sort of Swiss bodices and white skirts, with full sleeves. At night they set up a "wild howling kind of ballad" accompanied by bagpipes—a serenade that took place, Lawrence discovered, nightly until Christmas. Most of his contacts with the peasants must have been through Orazio Cervi, who had learned a little English when he had worked in London as a model. Orazio was a "queer creature—so nice, but slow and tentative," Lawrence told Rosalind Popham Baynes. After trying the rigors of an authentic peasant existence, Lawrence was moved to sympathize with the plight of his host, a permanent resident of the locale: "Poor Orazio!" His blood knowledge notwithstanding, this young man who lives as Pancrazio in *The Lost Girl* was to fall ill and perish less than three years later.

Before a week had passed, Lawrence confessed that Picinisco, though "beautiful beyond words," was "*so* primitive, and *so* cold, that I thought we should die." Lawrence remembered an offer Compton Mackenzie had extended in 1914 and he now wrote to inquire whether he and Frieda might take his cottage on Capri. Mackenzie replied that he had just lent the cottage to the Francis Brett Youngs, but promised that he and Young* would find cheap and comfortable accommodations for them if they would come anyway. On the Saturday before Christmas, it snowed throughout the day, and the Lawrences had to spend a snowbound holiday shivering in the kitchen. On the following Monday, Lawrence and Frieda arose at dawn, put their sparse belongings onto the back of an ass, and struggled the five miles to Latina through the drifts and over the "wild river with its great white bed of boulders . . . pale and frizzy from the ice." (The asphalt road did not exist then.) There they caught the post omnibus to the Cassino station ten miles distant. On the way south, Lawrence caught a glimpse of the snow-capped monastery of Monte Cassino, "crouching there above," but a visit would have to wait until a more propitious time. What had started as an adventure had ended not quite totally as a fiasco: from those icy mountains and memorable days Lawrence carried away the impressions that would be expressed, later under a Sicilian sun, as the finale of *The Lost Girl*.

The train reached Naples in time for them to catch the

---

*Francis Brett Young, the author of several novels and some of the best neo-Georgian poetry.

three o'clock boat to Capri. As the "poor little iron tub of a steamer" left the bay, the sea rose, and by darkness, when they came into the shallow port of Capri after five hours of wallowing, the seas ran so high that the small boats could not put out to land them—when a boat approached to take them off, "it almost hopped on to our deck, and then fell back into an abysmal gulf of darkness, amid yells unparalleled almost even in Italy." There was nothing to do but go back and seek the semishelter of Sorrento, there to spend the night rolling at anchor "with a lot of spewing Italians." Neither Lawrence nor Frieda became sick, and a few hours later they were able to enjoy the magnificent red dawn that came up over the Mediterranean as they once more pushed across to Capri. There they were "hurled like sacks" into the curvetting boats and hauled up the funicular to the town itself.

As good as Mackenzie's word, Francis Brett Young found them two large, well-furnished, inexpensive rooms, with three balconies, and a kitchen to share, on the top floor of an old palazzo owned by Carlo Ferraro, the island's pharmacist. The Lawrences had to climb a "staircase like a prison, not a palace," but they were more than pleased with their quarters on the "villa-stricken, two-humped chunk of limestone." Lawrence wrote gleefully to Cynthia Asquith:

> My palace roof, where F. and I hang out the washing, is the very saddle of Capri on which we ride the island . . . One bestrides the narrow world without being a Colossus.

High above the narrow streets, they could look out over the "tiny jungle of Capri town . . . the piazza, the little square, where all the island life throbs," and across the little gulf of the street by the end balcony, "the comical whitewashed cathedral." Just below was Morgano's Café, where

the artists and the expatriates congregated for aperitifs
before lunch and for conversation in the evenings.

On clear days their gaze could sweep to the right as far as
Ischia and the "exquisite long curve" of the Bay of Naples,
with Vesuvius rolling "a white glittering smoke level on the
wing," and to the left, over the "wide open Mediterranean,"
whose waters "unfolded like fresh petals" in the brilliant
sunshine. The sea itself and the bathing beaches were a
short, steep mile away. The days were full of hot sunshine
or "stormy, blowy, rainy—but not cold," though on occasion
they required a fire in the evenings. The sunsets were spectacular and the flowers bloomed in profuse color.

After Picinisco, life in Capri was "pleasant and bohemian."
There was the maid Liberata to take care of the rooms,
leaving most of the day for diversion. To Cynthia Asquith
he wrote, "There is always a fly in the ointment, be it even
spikenard, always a hair in the soup. So—*dolce far* [sic] *niente*.
Here I sit at the top of my palace, and do nothing—sweet
nothing,* except go out to lunch, or walk from one end of
the island to the other." To another friend he wrote in the
same vein:

> The days pass rather lazily. I ought really to
> work. But one loses the desire. Now the
> weather is sunny again, we think of starting
> bathing. Italy is a lazy country. One meets peo-
> ple, and lounges till the next meal: and so life
> passes.

---

*Not precisely. In January (1920), shortly after arriving on Capri, Law-
rence resumed work on "Education of the People" (*Phoenix*), part of an
ambitious but never realized project. In *A Bibliography of D. H. Lawrence*, p.
163, Warren Roberts says that Lawrence noted in his diary that he had
begun the essay "at the Palazzo Ferraro in Capri on 15 June 1920," but
there must be a mistake somewhere, for Lawrence on that day was in
Taormina.

Among the people to meet were "heaps of cosmopolitan dwellers—English, American, Russian by the dozen, Dutch, German, Dane," but Lawrence soon grew bored with them, preferring the company of Italians or of his Romanian neighbor who shared the kitchen. One Saturday he climbed the two miles to the top peak of the island, Monte Solaro, with his new friend, and they spent "fierce evenings in a discussion of idealistic philosophy, I in my bad English-Italian, larded with French, he in his furious Romanian-Italian, peppered with both French and German."* Compton Mackenzie reports one such occasion:

> The charcoal stove in the kitchen was a source of pleasure to Lawrence because he had mastered the art of cooking with charcoal and enjoyed a demonstration of his skill. He [the Romanian], too was proud of his skill with a charcoal stove and used to compete with Lawrence. Francis and I called once when they were in the middle of an argument about Plotinus, both of them fanning away energetically at the *fornello* while they were arguing. Frieda Lawrence had retired to the bedroom; the kitchen and the sitting-room were full of the fumes of charcoal and neo-Platonism; Lawrence's red beard was black, Francis and I hurried to open the windows before we and the two philosophic cooks were asphyxiated.

Another time, he and Frieda went with Maria Ferraro, their *signora*, and some Italian friends to look at the villa lo Esmeraldo, a beautiful house above the sea. Lawrence

---

*He may have worked his way into *Women in Love* as the drunken Romanian who gives "the most marvelous address," partly in Romanian, at Fanny Bath's studio.

wanted some land under his feet and the villa could be let for a thousand francs a month—he hoped that Cynthia Asquith would take it, then rent an apartment to him. Before long, the party had gathered wood, lit up the fireplace in the drawing room, and after pausing for tea, danced on the marble floor while someone played the piano until the sun went down. From all accounts the strange, stiff Englishman accepted the Italians easily and in turn was accepted by them.

Though his letters say very little more about his idle hours, Lawrence could not have avoided the sometime company of the island's familiar figures and its winter guests— nor would he always have wanted to There was Dr. Axel Munthe, the fashionable Swedish physician with whom Ottoline Morrell had conducted a youthful premarital affair. His famous San Michele commanded the finest view of the island and was a gathering place for persons of renown. There Lawrence may have listened to the grave courtesies of the composer Respighi and the provocative theories of Filippo Marinetti, the founder of the artistic movement called "Futurism" (which Lawrence seems to have taken seriously in his poetic practice and translated into the "pollyanalytics" of *Women in Love*). From time to time, Reggie Turner and Norman Douglas, whose *South Wind* was still read avidly by the residents, would come over from Florence.

The Lawrences were frequently in the company of Francis Brett Young and his wife Jessica; Julian and Juliette Huxley and Maria Nys, the Belgian woman who would become the wife of Aldous Huxley. And Mary Cannan, whom they had met in England, called on them regularly and they on her. Already part of the island's life, she alternately entertained and horrified Lawrence with stories of scandal that would have made "Suetonius . . . blush to his heels"—Lawrence inferred that rape, lesbianism, homosexuality, and nude dancing were rife on Capri. She also regaled the Lawrences with the intimate details of her life with her first husband, Sir James Barrie, then with the novelist Gilbert Cannan, whom she had recently divorced. Lawrence stoutly defended her as "one of the decentest people on the island."

There were others whose company Lawrence enjoyed. For instance, he liked to visit John Ellingham Brooks, one of the first Englishmen to establish residence on Capri, arriving there as a young classical scholar in the 1890s. He shared the Villa Cercola with Somerset Maugham and E. F. Benson, another writer. In this arrangement, Brooks occupied the villa permanently but his cotenants could come and stay whenever they wished. Brooks used to play his piano by the hour and Lawrence, who was also partial to that instrument, must have enjoyed hearing him perform. When he returned to Capri some years later, Lawrence renewed his acquaintance with the old beachcomber.

It is possible that he may have met Maugham at that time, though there is no mention of such a meeting in the letters. Later, he did meet Maugham in Mexico and concluded that Maugham was a "narrow-gutted 'artist' with a stutter." And he struck up a friendship with an Italian named Ferdinando di Chiara and his American wife Anna. Harry Moore thinks that this couple may have been the prototypes for Manfredi and Nan del Torre, whose salon serves as a background for two chapters in *Aaron's Rod*. This slightly ironic portrayal did not keep them from having lunch with Lawrence in New York or seeing him later in Bandol.

However, his closest associate of this period was Compton Mackenzie, already a successful novelist, who had suggested the possibility of Capri to Lawrence. Shortly after his arrival, Lawrence attended a New Year's celebration at Morgano's —primarily a "barbaric Italian affair," with bands of young men singing weird unintelligible ballads and performing tarantellas to a grunting kind of music. Toward midnight, Mackenzie pushed himself into the limelight, ordering champagne for his friends and the employees trimming the holiday tree in the face of the Americans, and in general, playing Joseph to his brethren. Lawrence and company— Frieda, Brooks, and an old Dutchman—sat at the other end of the table, feeling ignored but amused at the spectacle of the self-conscious Americans trying to look "wine and womanish" and Mackenzie "in a pale blue suit to match his eyes" acting the role of the "bounteous English Signore" before the slightly contemptuous Italians (in Lawrence's fiction, the Italian types are often silent and quietly scornful of the rich Anglo-Saxons who behave self-consciously or inauthentically—though in this instance, Mackenzie maintains that Lawrence read all sorts of dark significance into his perfectly normal conduct at Morgano's).

But Lawrence forgave what he regarded at first as Mackenzie's frivolity ("one feels the generation of actors behind him, and can't be quite serious"), and though he continued to disapprove of Mackenzie's silk pajamas and ties, his woman's velour hat, and his aesthetic walk, there developed between the two writers a reciprocal fondness that endured until Lawrence satirized Mackenzie as Cathcart in "The Man Who Loved Islands." Mackenzie liked Lawrence's originality, his flair for finding delight in the world, and his innocent and interesting eccentricity, and Lawrence liked Mackenzie's graciousness, intelligence, and style. Frieda, "bubbling from the depths of her Teutonic bonhomie," one day told Mackenzie that she didn't know anyone whom Lawrence had liked as much as he liked Mackenzie. Soon he was visiting the Lawrences in town almost as frequently as Lawrence was calling upon him at the Casa Solitaria, his magnificent (rented) villa perched on the rocks overlooking the sea.

"We used to have great afternoons at Casa Solitaria," says Mackenzie nostalgically, "with Brooks thumping away at the Erard Grand and Lawrence and me singing Sally in Our Alley and Barbara Allen. Francis [Young], who had a perfect ear, used to sit looking slightly pained by the way Lawrence and I were singing in different keys." At other times, the two of them talked "by the hour" about going to the South Seas together and collaborating on a travel book about the region. They had read in the *Pacific Pilot* a description of the Kermadec Islands which seemed perfect for Rananim, and part of their plan was to take a selected group of people to recolonize these islands four hundred miles north of Auckland (they had been evacuated owing to volcanic eruptions). Mackenzie wrote to Pember Reeves, then the New Zealand high commissioner, requesting him to ascertain the views of his government about such a project. Mackenzie learned that the islands had already been leased to a New Zealander, but he did not give up his efforts to raise the money for the ketch that would transport Lawrence, himself, and the company to paradise—until Martin Secker opposed the plan. Lawrence was not to see those romantic waters until his return sailing from Ceylon. Once more Rananim proved to be only a dream.

That winter Lawrence was working on *Fantasia of the Unconscious* and Mackenzie let him borrow the L. C. Smith typewriter on which only the red half of the ribbon was still usable. The original typescript of the book was done in red, a color scheme that Lawrence said, to the puzzlement of Mackenzie, had been helpful to him in the composition. In honor of Mackenzie's thirty-seventh birthday, he brought the typewriter back to Casa Solitaria, and Mackenzie reports that he was much moved by the sight of Lawrence's slight figure coming down the steps of the villa that sunny morning, one arm holding the L. C. Smith atop his head, the other carrying a bottle of Benedictine, a gift to Mackenzie, disdaining to hire a *facchino* to bring the heavy machine the two miles from the Palazzo Ferraro. On another occasion, Mackenzie listened to a gloomy Lawrence expound on James Joyce. Lawrence was walking along the cliff path to Casa Solitaria, carrying in a string bag an orange and a banana and under his arm copies of *The Little Review* containing

serialized sections of *Ulysses*. Lawrence had been reading the
novel: "This *Ulysses* muck is more disgusting than Casanova,"
he said. "I must show that it can be done without muck." Were
Lady Chatterley and her lover, Mackenzie wondered, conceived at that moment on Capri?

Whether the novel was born then or not (it wasn't), the
reading of *Ulysses* set Lawrence off to talking about sex. Mackenzie had not heard the theory of blood consciousness, and one
day while Lawrence was discussing the ancient Greek philos-
ophers, he suddenly stopped and began to argue that men
must give up thinking with their minds. "'What we have to
learn is to think here,'" he affirmed solemnly in "that high
pitched voice of his with its slight Midlands accent." As he said
this, he bent over to point a finger at his fly buttons, to Mackenzie's embarrassment and to the obvious surprise of other people strolling on the piazza. Lawrence apparently was not
amused when Mackenzie told him that an old *guardia* might
approach him and advise, "*Queste cose, signore, si fanno in casa
privata*." ("This kind of thing is done in the privacy of the
home.")

At another time, he told Mackenzie that despite his concen-
tration on the genital organs, he was worried about his inabil-
ity to attain consummation simultaneously with Frieda—an
incompatibility that made him feel that his marriage was
imperfect despite all the two of them had endured for its sake.
Mackenzie tried to cheer him up by pointing out that such a
happy coincidence was rare, but Lawrence became increasingly depressed about what he insisted was the only evidence
of a perfect union. "I believe that the nearest I've ever come to
perfect love was with a young coal-miner when I was about
sixteen," he allegedly declared to Mackenzie. That morning,
Mackenzie reports, Lawrence went on and on about the need
for people "to think with their genital organs instead of their
minds," and he praised the Etruscans, who he was convinced
"thought with their genital organs." Lawrence may well have

been pulling Mackenzie's leg, but such levity at his expense did not stop Mackenzie from suggesting *Women in Love* as a title for Lawrence's new novel or from encouraging Martin Secker to publish it.

Despite Mackenzie's hospitality, from time to time Lawrence had to flee the confinement of the lotus-eaters' life on "Little Babel" (as he sometimes referred to Capri), and he would sometimes slip over to Naples for the day, refreshing himself by the sight of the misty cliffs ahead and hanging over the side of the steamer when it paused for passengers at Massa and Sorrento, to watch the "watery Neapolitan people" as they clambered in and out of their little boats "in their native trustful way." At another time, prevented from working by postal and railway strikes that held up the manuscript of "A Mixed Marriage" (a second title for *The Lost Girl*, replacing "The Insurrection of Miss Houghton"), he took Frieda on an extended holiday to Amalfi, where they could "look around for a little house." Only big ones were vacant. But the sheer rocky coast was so beautiful that "one sheds one's avatar, and recovers a lost self, Mediterranean, anterior to us." Lawrence would return to the area later, to continue his quest for the lost Mediterranean self. But it became amply clear to the Lawrences that they did not have the means to settle so close to the main tourist trail in Italy.

Lawrence's most momentous trip to the mainland was that strange pilgrimage to the abbey of Monte Cassino in late February of 1920. Lawrence had wanted to visit the medieval abbey ever since Magnus had put the idea in his head back in Florence, and when another invitation came from Magnus at Monte Cassino, Lawrence determined to go even though it meant an exhausting day's travel each way for a stay of only three nights. In the black dark of a February morning, Lawrence got up, made a little coffee in the spirit lamp, and groping his way down "the smelly dark stone stairs of the old palazzo," started out on a journey into himself at the medieval monastery. Magnus extended nervous hospitality to his guest, and the guest master, Don Bernardo, "good-looking, gentle," showed him the treasures of the monastery, including the casket of Benvenuto Cellini.

Lawrence refers to the visit rather casually in a letter of March 20: "Montecassino is wonderful—and the monks are charming to one. But it seems pathetic, now, in its survival, so frail and hardly vital any more. Of course it should be *feudal:* like a great fortress hanging over the plain. What is it now it is divested of power and turned into a sort of museum where the forty monks linger on?" However, anyone who wishes to understand Lawrence's frame of mind and spiritual crisis at this time should read his superb account of that experience in his introduction to the memoirs of Magnus. In the cold stillness of his cell the following morning, in "the poignant grip of the past, the grandiose, violent past of the Middle Ages, when blood was strong," he gazed down on the distant plain which seemed to represent the world of the present with all its venality and mechanization he so despised. The monastery beckoned as a symbol of bygone days into which there might be escape— the tranquillity of San Tommaso, the warmth of the Church of the Dove. "To see all this from the monastery, where the Middle Ages live on is a sort of agony, like Tithonus, and cannot die, this was almost a violation of my soul, made almost a wound." But Lawrence refused the temptation of the retreat, and like Hans Castorp, descended from the mountain to wrestle with his destiny.

On the way back, watching fat Italians eating macaroni in the dining car of the Rome–Naples train, "with the big glass windows steamed opaque and the rain beating outside," Lawrence let himself be carried away, "away from the monastery, away from M[agnus], away from everything." On the little steamer at Naples port, he sat in "a bit of sunshine" and felt that the world had come to an end and that his heart was broken: "the steamer seemed to be making its way away from the old world, that came to another end in me."

By the time Lawrence had resumed his activities on Capri, the island life had lost the last of its flavor for him. His dissatisfactions were new only in degree. Even at the beginning of his stay in January (1920) Lawrence had looked upon Capri as "sympathetic for a time . . . but not an abiding place." He talks about going back to Germany or venturing off to an African farm near Nairobi or colonizing a South Sea island. As winter wore on the Capriotes became decreasingly cordial—"they had a strange grudge against us"—and Italy, he tells Amy Lowell in a letter thanking her for a gift of money, "isn't what it was, a cheerful insouciant land." On the practical side, living at a winter resort was "frightfully expensive . . . butter 20 francs, wine 3 francs a litre the cheapest—sugar 8 francs a kilo—a porter expects ten francs for bringing one's luggage from the sea" (apparently the Lawrences' lost luggage had just arrived). He had definitely tired of insular life and had grown annoyed by the congestion of Europeans—"too many for this tiny island." And the colony of English intellectuals, whose antics had amused him at first, was now making him "as spiteful as the rest of Capri" and turning the island into a "stewpot of semi-literary cats." Capri became anathema to the Lawrences when Frieda discovered that one of her diamond rings had been stolen from her room. "One shouldn't have diamonds violà tout!" commented Lawrence.

Chapter 5

LATE in February (the twenty-sixth, according to Ada Lawrence Clarke), Lawrence took a trip to Sicily with the Francis Brett Youngs to see the temples at Agrigentum and possibly to find a house for the next year. Mackenzie notes that Lawrence on his return did not sound impressed by Sicily—Francis Young says it was because his hat blew away when they were looking at the temples—but one of his letters argues otherwise: "Sicily, tall, forever rising up to her gem-like summits, all golden in dawn, and always glamorous . . ." In fact, Lawrence almost took a house in Syracuse and then in Girgenti (which Magnus had recommended to him), but when the striking sulfur miners started to throw stones at the strangers, Lawrence hastily headed for the safety of Taormina. Lady Ottoline Morrell had spent part of her childhood there and she must have told Lawrence about the ruins and the gardens where life no doubt had been lived passionately some two thousand years earlier. Lawrence fell for the spectacular setting (Magnus hated it) of Taormina, and his eye fell on a *villino*, Fontana Vecchia, in a relatively isolated location at the end of a narrow dirt road, with a garden shaded by olive, almond, lemon, and peach trees, and a roomy upper floor overlooking the sea, available for twenty-five pounds per annum when the occupant, an unfriendly English-woman, moved out on the first of March. As further recommendations, it had been built by wealthy cousins of Robert

Trevelyan's wife, and it came equipped with a blue Dutch kitchen and a family of peasant proprietors named Cacopardo. Shortly after his return to Capri, Lawrence borrowed fifty francs from Mackenzie and, escorted by Mary Cannan, he and Frieda boarded the *vaporetto* to Naples en route to Sicily. Lawrence must have gone ahead to Messina, and there his train was met by a "wall of mist . . . rolling up the Straits," the first sign of what he hinted were "dark influences" enveloping the ancient island. At Taormina, he concluded the leasing terms with the proprietor, Francesco Cacopardo,* who would be living on the ground floor with his mother Grazia, his brother Carmelo, and his sister Ciccia. He then went down to the seaside station at Giardini to meet the *accelerato* carrying Frieda and Mary Cannan (but not their trunks, which Lawrence had to fetch from Catania the following day).

The first evening in Sicily the trio spent at the Hotel Bristol, and possibly the second as well, but by the first Monday in March, the Lawrences were comfortably installed in the Fontana Vecchia, and that evening as he watched Etna puffing fire from its peak, he wrote to Mackenzie:

> Frieda loves the house, so does Mary—do you imagine the balcony at night?—the Plough pitching headlong, but the sea on the left, terribly falling, and Taormina in a rift on the right fuming tremulously between the jaws of dark-

---

*Later known to Lawrence by the affectionate nickname of Cicio or Ciccio Moddu, the landlord became the model for "cat-like" Cicio in *The Lost Girl*, which received its final touches at the Fontana Vecchia. Lawrence asked Secker (February 8, 1927) to spell his name with three *c*'s in the reprint. The landlord's given name, Francesco, also pops up in the novel: "Tall and handsome and well-coloured [he] might be Italian." Grazia, the waitress in the Post Restaurant in *The Lost Girl*, may be based on Cacopardo's mother.

ness—I wonder if I shall write—Heaven save us
all!

During the first fortnight in Taormina, Lawrence felt
"twinges of heimweh or nostalgia for the north," but before
long he declared himself to be "wavering south." The pink
stucco farmhouse high above the Mediterranean, sighting
east toward Africa and west to the crest of Calabria where
the straits began to close in, became his "tower of the sea,"
and Lawrence decided that he would spend at least a year
among the almond trees and olives. "I've reached my limit
for the moment," he wrote Mackenzie, "like a spent bird
straggling down the straits."

The house stands on the outskirts of town, a healthy fifteen minutes' walk, and the Lawrences must have led a relatively quiet life. After the capers on Capri, Lawrence was
indifferent to the cosmopolitan ambience that the foreign
colony offered in the hotels and *pensiones* of Taormina. "I
wish Taormina village weren't there, that's all—with Timeo,
Domenico, and Villaolatri," he complains good-naturedly to
Mackenzie. He visited Mary Cannan occasionally at the
"marvellous suite she had discovered in an old people's
home." On his invitation, two young painters whom he had
met in Rome—Jan Juta and Alan Insole—had come to Taormina and he made friends with a "slit-eyed Dutch woman"
named Hubrecht. But the Lawrences stayed close to home.
Mary Cannan came to tea regularly and it is more than likely
that the Lawrences played host to the Honorable Alexander
Nelson-Hood, the Duke of Bronte, who owned a manor estate at Maniacci, at the foot of Mount Etna. If he did indeed
visit the Lawrences, it may have been the ducal appearance
he liked to affect at times which gave rise to the rumor that
the king of England had called on them incognito. According
to his landlord, Lawrence entertained local magistrates at
breakfast. On one occasion, the mayor of Taormina, Fran-

cesco Atenasio, arrived in time to see Frieda toss a plate of fried potatoes at her husband, and departed without touching the ham and eggs, buttered toast, and milk that Lawrence usually served his early guests.

Under the sun of Sicily, free of the "soul-stiffening one must perform against a legion of windy-watery fools," Lawrence once more tapped into a rich, free vein of creativity. As he wrote, he could gaze out from his balcony over "the green and pleasant hills" toward smoking Etna, "deep hooded with snow" or sit before the small shower of his fountain "in a sort of little cave-place down the garden." Probably the story "Sun," though written later at Spotorno, was conceived among these surroundings ("[there was] a spring issuing out of a little cavern, where the old Sicules had drunk before the Greeks came; and a grey goat bleating, stabled in an ancient tomb, with all the niches empty. There was the scent of mimosa, and beyond, the snow of the volcano"), and some of the most lyrical poems in *Birds, Beasts and Flowers* ("Peace," "Tropic," "Southern Night," "The Ass," and the two goat poems) took form as well.

As the weather became warmer, he would go down to the sweet-smelling lemon grove and pick baskets of *nespoli*, an apricotlike fruit which Frieda put into her pies. He enjoyed chattering with the Cacopardos and before long, Italian phrases were creeping into his correspondence (and poems) and he was soon calling Francesco by his familiar name of Moddu. He exulted to Fritz Krenkow: "I like Sicily—oh, so much better than Capri. It is so green and living." And to Koteliansky, he confides: "It is very lovely here. I feel I shall never come north again."

Frieda was no less delighted by this southern scene. In their "little blue kitchen," with Lawrence lending a hand, she made "cakes and tarts, big and little, sweet pies and meat pies, and put them on the sideboard in the dining room and called them Mrs. Beeton's show." On Sundays, she would prepare roast beef, baked potatoes, spinach, and apple pie, and sometimes, Lawrence, who loved to putter in the kitchen, made "heavenly chocolate cakes . . . and exquisite rock cakes." If the spirit of Italy was not in their cuisine, it was to be found just beyond the window, where life moved with the slow pulse of Mediterranean nature. "Along our rocky road," Frieda writes, "the peasants rode past into the hills on their donkeys, singing loudly; the shepherds drove their goats along, playing their reed pipes as in the days of the Greeks." In these surroundings, they both sensed the presence of many civilizations: "Greek and Moorish and Norman and beyond into the dim past." The natural flow of time in simple space reminded both of them of the rhythms to which they had submitted their daily lives at Lake Garda and at Fiascherino.

Later, Lawrence was to observe that the "intense watchful malice" of the inland Sicilians was "infinitely worse than any police system, infinitely more killing to the soul and passionate body" (from the introduction to his translation of *Mastro Don Gesualdo* by Giovanni Verga), but at that time he and Frieda were enchanted with the "undying beauty of Sicily and the Greek world, a morning beauty, that has something miraculous in it, of purple anemones and cyclamens, and sumach and olive trees and the place where Persephone came above-world, bringing back spring." In *Birds, Beasts and Flowers*, these benign images become the cutting instruments for Lawrence's feelings about Mediterranean savages emerging from the mists of history ("Sicilian Cyclamens"), mythical/modern wives who feud with their husbands over "rights for women" ("Purple Anemones"), and young Sicilian Socialists who swagger along the Corso, the main street of Taormina, on Sunday mornings angering English expatriates like himself with their bolshevik belligerency ("Hibiscus and Salvia Flowers").

Sometime in April, according to Mackenzie, Lawrence was called away from his bucolic refuge by a piece of complicated business: back in England, Martin Secker had offered to publish *Women in Love* and *The Rainbow* at favorable royalty rates. However, Secker wanted to bring out *Women* before undertaking to republish *The Rainbow*,* and part of the problem was that the typescript in America, from which Lawrence wanted Secker to set, did not match the one in his possession. According to Secker (letter to Mackenzie, April 1920), the American typescript may have had "all the best bits taken out and a lot of lesbianism written in" by someone other than the author himself. Secker thought that Lawrence might go mad if he did not have something in print soon and apparently the visit to London helped to preserve his sanity.

Upon his return to Taormina, Lawrence found two invitations waiting for him—one from friends in Syracuse to visit that ancient city and the other from Alexander Nelson-Hood to spend a few days at his ducal manor house at Bronte. Lawrence decided to combine both visits into a single journey.

The estate of Bronte had belonged to the hospital of Palermo until the Neapolitans had given the income of it to Lord Horatio Nelson—a gift of about eighteen thousand ducats per annum, which Nelson called "magnificent and worthy of a king"—and made him Duca di Bronte ("because," says Lawrence, "he hanged a few of them"). Nelson had great visions of improving the estate so that he could make all Sicilians "bless the day I was placed among them," but there must have been few blessings to count, for the

---

*Not until February of 1926 was Secker able to bring out a crown octavo edition of *The Rainbow*, from unbound sheets imported from Seltzer in New York and bound exactly like the other Lawrence novels—an edition, by the way, not recorded in Roberts's *Bibliography of D. H. Lawrence*.

dukes of Bronte, by the late nineteenth century, were employing their own private police to protect their rights of property. According to Carlo Levi in *Words and Stones*, the farmworkers at Bronte were among the most miserable in all Italy and were still fighting the daily war against the persisting feudal attitudes of the duchy. Lawrence was only partially aware of this history and could have had no substantial moral reasons for not accepting the invitation, though later on the soul-grinding poverty of the Sicilian peasants would stir his profoundest sympathies.

On April 24 or 25, accompanied by Jan Juta, his sister Réné Hansard, and Alan Insole, a young Welsh painter, the Lawrences caught the coastal train for Syracuse. From the window of their car, the view was glorious, and the group could admire the purple anemones blowing in the fields and the green corn waving in the wind. As they passed the "rocks of Polyphemus off the coast near Catania, Lawrence half expected to see the galleys of Odysseus plowing through the surf—at least so he says. In the harbor of Syracuse, there were fishing smacks with eyes painted on the bows, and in the streets were carts whose sides the native artists had enlivened with scenes depicting local legends. He marveled at the great quarry of Latomia, where the Greeks had gotten the stone for the ancient city, and he told his sister Ada in a letter that Syracuse was a "wonderful place," despite an uncomfortable night at the hotel (described in the poem called "The Mosquito").

But Lawrence remembered above all how Réné Hansard, "fortified with a hamper of food and a spirit-lamp," could convert the railway car into a "live little temporary home" with the aplomb of a colonist. Lawrence worked this memory into a chapter of the almost-completed *Aaron's Rod*, in which the youthful travelers on the train to Florence "pitch camp in the midst of civilization." Jan Juta told me that Lawrence used him as the model for one of the young painters in that scene and that his sister Réné is recognizable in *St. Mawr*.

On the journey back from Syracuse to Bronte, the party got out for a picnic at Randazzo,* an ancient village on the slope of Etna where the railway line halts. While awaiting the duke's emissaries who were to pick them up, the party explored the town. Lawrence was captivated by the houses of black-lava stone and the church interiors of contrasting white marble. After a while, they were met by a "band of exhausted Sicilian shepherds with bandy legs," costumed as the Vatican's Swiss Guard, who had come to fetch them. As the party approached the manor on muleback, they were greeted by the duke himself, who scrutinized them suspiciously through his monocle, and by his sister, who wore a bees' nest on her head in imitation of the queen. Lawrence liked the place, with its broad stables, its private chapel, and its spacious and shady grounds, but he took exception to "*M'le Duc*," noting ironically that "money maketh a man: even if he was a monkey to start with."

Lawrence's letters about the journey are lyrical, but the duke and his retinue—who inspired a satiric scenario which he scrapped—made him itch to be back "in our own house above the almond trees, and the sea in the cove below . . . the lovely dawn-sea in front, where the sun rose with a splendour like trumpets every morning, and me rejoicing like madness in this dawn, day-dawn, life-dawn, the dawn which is Greece, which is me." After a stay of four days, the Lawrences were back at Fontana Vecchia.

But into this paradise "suddenly crept the serpent." Early one morning, Lawrence heard a noise on the stairs from the lower terrace and went to investigate. There, looking up at him with a frightened face, was Magnus. He had uncere-

---

*Lawrence in a letter to Mackenzie (*My Life and Times*, p. 183), says that "we were away at Randazzo for 3 days," but seems to be referring to his stay at Bronte.

moniously fled from Monte Cassino, he said, ten minutes before the *carabiniere* had arrived in search of the *Americano* who had written a rubber check to an Anzio innkeeper. The *Americano* happened to be Magnus. In order to escape detection on the train, he had had to hide himself in the WC until Naples. With only a few lire in his pocket, he had been waiting at the San Domenico Hotel (the most expensive in Taormina) for Lawrence's return and guidance. A sophisticated if indigent aristocrat like himself, he hinted, knew how to appreciate the advantages of the Fontana Vecchia. Lawrence, who sensed that Magnus had become a perennial parasite, ignored the hint and gave Magnus a hundred lire.

The following day Magnus appeared again: could Lawrence advance him money on the manuscript of his memoirs, which they had gone over together while Lawrence was staying at Monte Cassino? He was so desperately broke that he could not pay his hotel bill. Lawrence offered to settle the bill if Magnus would move to an inexpensive *pensione*. Piqued, nevertheless Magnus took a cheap room with a townsman named Pancrazio Malenga. The next day he asked Lawrence if he would be good enough to fetch the manuscript and the personal belongings which he had left behind at Monte Cassino in his precipitous departure. Lawrence flatly refused to undertake such an arduous journey and hoped that this refusal might drive off Magnus. But when Magnus, only slightly crestfallen, continued to hang on, Lawrence felt that he was becoming "an intolerable weight and like a clot of dirt over everything."

Nearly two weeks passed before Lawrence was again sucked into the affairs of Magnus. There had been an altercation between Magnus and his landlord. According to Magnus, Don Bernardo, the guestmaster at Monte Cassino, had forwarded a letter containing a check for seven guineas, but had written erroneously on the envelope "Orazio" Malenga instead of "Pancrazio." The post office had refused to deliver the letter and had returned it to the sender. Words followed and Magnus accused Malenga of insulting his good name. He would leave for Egypt immediately and never return to accursed Italy. Malenga, however, had another version of the disagreement: Magnus had been living like a king at his expense and had paid him only with promises. "He says always it is coming, it is coming, today, tomorrow, today, tomorrow. *E non viene mai niente.*" When Malenga had said this to Magnus, he had taken umbrage and without explanation was preparing to depart. Where was he, Pancrazio Malenga, to get his money?

Once more Lawrence settled the bill for Magnus, this time with the help of a small fund that Jan Juta had collected from his friends for the purpose of helping Magnus out of his troubles, and both Lawrence and Juta breathed with relief when Magnus left for Malta en route to Alexandria in early May. Juta, en route to Taormina earlier in the spring, had picked up the Magnus manuscript at the abbey and had delivered it to Lawrence, advising him to cut and reduce the parts of the text which Juta thought Magnus had manufactured out of his fantasies. According to his own account in "Accumulated Mail" (*Phoenix*), Lawrence had to rewrite about half of the manuscript, cutting out much of the obscenity that Juta says was in the original, and, under pressure from Magnus, had undertaken to write an introduction that would insure at least a small readership through the attraction of his name.

It was about the time of the Magnus affair that Lawrence was finishing off *The Lost Girl*, and perhaps to commemorate the memory of Magnus as well as the month of his departure, Lawrence decided to call the shifty American theatrical manager whom he had modeled on Magnus, "Mr. May." And if Lawrence was looking for a name for the character who was to be based on Orazio Cervi, his landlord at Picinisco, Taormina provided him with Pancrazio.

Lawrence was still dreaming exuberantly about a voyage to the South Seas (Mackenzie had his eye on the "perfect craft" for that purpose, he wrote) when Mary Cannan, who was madly keen to visit Malta, begged the Lawrences to accompany her and even offered to pay their passage. Lawrence had just completed one novel and had started another, and had arranged the publication of *Women in Love* in America through Seltzer (despite Gilbert Cannan's warning that the firm was bound to go bankrupt) and in England through Secker, who wanted to bring it out under the less provocative title of *The Sisters*. He was in the mood to travel, and now he could afford the luxury of a holiday owing to an unexpected windfall.

Earlier that April, Gilbert Cannan, fresh from a lecture tour of the United States, had come "express" from Rome to chastise Lawrence for a letter "slandering his Gwen" (Gwen Mond, the wife of Henry Mond, later 2nd Baron Melchett, with whom Cannan was apparently having an affair). Lawrence wrote to Mackenzie about this brief encounter:

> The main upshot is that in his indignation he disgorged a cheque for £75 SEVENTY FIVE POUNDS STERLING as the equivalent of $300 which he had collected from Americans for me. Benone! Fortune had it that for once Mary wasn't here to tea; and that he had taken a room at Domenico as being a little grander than Timeo [where Mary Cannan was staying then]. He is tout américain—L'Americanisato! pocket book thick, fat, bulging with 1,000 Lire notes—"these beastly hotels"—and "Oh yes, picked up quite a lot of money over there"— "Oh yes, they seemed to take to me quite a lot." "Yes, have promised a quantity of people I'll go back this Fall."

After two hours of conversation, they parted "as friends

who will never speak to each other again." Lawrence dismissed him as an "imbecile," not knowing that in a year or two, Cannan would be certified insane and would spend the last thirty years of his life in a private asylum in Richmond, thinking that it was his own house.

The "wretchedness" of the Magnus affair and the exasperation of the Cannan encounter dwindled into memory as the Lawrences "on a hot, hot Thursday" sat in the train running south, the four and a half hours' journey to Syracuse en route to Malta. At Syracuse, a steamer strike delayed them and the trip "trailed off into the town, to the Grand Hotel," a rather dreary old Italian place just opposite the port, "with many bloodstains of squashed mosquitoes on the bedroom walls." Despite the "vile mosquitoes," the port of Syracuse exerted its fascination again:

> The sun went down behind that lovely, sinuous
> sky-line, the harbour water was gold and red,
> the people promenaded in thick streams under
> the pomegranate trees and hibiscus trees. Arabs
> in white burnouses and fat Turks in red and
> black alpaca long coats strolled also—waiting
> for the steamer.

The next afternoon at lunch, the porter brought Lawrence a letter. Impossible, thought Lawrence. But he had not reckoned with the omnipresence of Magnus. He was staying at the other hotel along the waterfront. "Dear Lawrence," he wrote:

> I saw you this morning, all three of you walking
> down the Via Nazionale, but you would not
> look at me. I have got my visas and everything
> ready. The strike of the steamboats has delayed
> me here. I am sweating blood. I have a last
> request to make of you. Can you let me have

> ninety lire, to make up what I need for my hotel
> bill? If I cannot have this I am lost . . . I am at the
> Casa Politi, passing every half-hour in agony.

Lawrence walked over to the Casa Politi under the broiling afternoon sun, but missed Magnus. That evening he turned up at Lawrence's hotel, the "picture of misery and endurance." As he told Lawrence of the trials he had endured, "his eyes swimming with tears," Lawrence once more bailed him out of trouble by giving him another hundred lire.

That evening Lawrence, Frieda, and Mary went on board the steamer bound for Malta. Shortly afterward, dressed "like the grandest gentleman on earth and followed by a porter with a barrow of luggage," Magnus made a grand entrance. A bit later, as Lawrence was leaning on the rail of the second-class deck, looking back on the lights of Syracuse sinking into the sea, Magnus appeared out of the darkness. "Well," he said, with his little smirk of a laugh, "Good-bye Italy . . . I begin to breathe free for the first time since I left the monastery! How awful it's been! But of course in Malta, I shall be all right. Don Bernardo has written to his friends there. They'll have everything ready for me that I want, and I can pay you back the money you so kindly lent me." After Magnus "strutted away," Lawrence looked over to the first-class deck and watched with reluctant admiration as Magnus, puffing on a big cigar, chatted airily with a commander of the British fleet.

The following morning, during debarkation in Valletta harbor, Magnus gave Lawrence a "condescending, affable nod" and ordered his porter with his luggage onto a boat, "quite superb and brisk." Lawrence was not in Valletta twenty-four hours before Magnus, as if by magic, once more materialized, this time on the Strada Reale, "strutting in a smart white duck suit, with a white pique cravat," wearing black shoes with his summer finery because his white boots had disappeared. Failure, it seems, had gone to his head.

After three days, Lawrence found himself bored with the "bone-dry, bone-bare, hideous landscape" of the island, "stark as a corpse, no trees, no bushes even; a fearful landscape, cultivated and weary with ages of weariness, and old weary houses here and there"; but the strike forced him to remain for eight days instead of the three planned. Don Bernardo's friends drove the Lawrence party around the island and Magnus did his best to make the enforced stay bearable. By the time Lawrence finally left Malta, Magnus had discovered a little place near Rabat and was busy establishing himself there. For several months thereafter, he wrote to Lawrence, extolling the marvels of Malta and urging him to return for a month's vacation. When Lawrence failed to respond to these epistles of entreaty, there came a pathetic card from Magnus: "I haven't had a letter from you, no news at all. I am afraid you are ill, and feel anxious. Do write." But Lawrence didn't want to write. That stopped the correspondence and there was to be no further word from Malta until that November.

By the beginning of June, Lawrence was back in Taormina. He had read the proofs of *Movements in European History* and had received the typescript of *The Lost Girl*, which had been typed in Rome for "the monstrous figure" of 1348 lire. He sent a carbon copy of the novel to an American publisher with his landlord, Ciccio Cacopardo, while Mackenzie picked up the original in Rome and took it to Secker in London (who wanted to call it *The Bitter Cherry*).

Apparently the Maltese mood carried back to Sicily. Soon after his arrival at the Fontana Vecchia, he is complaining that Italy is *"very expensive"* and that the Italians are really "rather low-bred swine nowadays: so different from what they were." Despite his complaints about rising costs and temperature, he could "bear Sicily better than anywhere

else." Gilbert Cannan's check gave him a comfortable financial margin, and to cope with the heat, Lawrence adopted the
native habit. His mood changes:

> I live in pyjamas, barefoot, all day, lovely hot
> days of bright sun and sea, but a cool wind
> through the straits. We do our own work—I
> prefer it, can't stand people about: so when the
> floors must be washed (gently washed merely)
> or when I must put my suit of pyjamas in the
> tub, behold me, *in puris naturalibus*, performing
> the menial labors of the day.

One day, when Lawrence was lounging about the garden
in his pajamas, a snake came to drink at the water trough.
Even though he had been warned that the golden snakes of
Sicily were venomous, he abided the presence of the reptile
until it put its head back into "the dreadful hole" that he
had come out of. Unable to control his human conditioning,
Lawrence threw a stick at the retreating form—and he says
in the poem "Snake," often regarded as his supreme achieve-
ment in verse, "thus missed his chance with one of the lords
of life."

The pleasures and risks of domestic and natural life notwithstanding, Lawrence was restless. On June 11, he writes
Mackenzie:

> With my mind's eye I see Nukahiva [the largest
> island of the Marquesas where, Lawrence
> believed, Herman Melville found "paradise"—
> *Studies in Classic American Literature*.] Ah God! Such
> a lovely sea here today, and a great white ship
> on the wind, making towards the South-East.
> I'd give my fingers to be off.

And on June 30, he is again writing to Mackenzie, this

time to express his enthusiasm about a ketch that they
dreamed about buying.

> The *Lavengro* of course thrills me to my marrow.
> Yes, I'd sail the Spanish Main in her. How big
> was Drake's ship? Is she steam as well as sails?
> How many men do you consider you'd want to
> run her? I pace out her length on the terrace
> below.

He concluded with a little verse:

> You can sell Capri. Anybody can have Capri.
> I'm glad she's not called the Bible of Spain.
> Round the world if need be.
> And round the world again—

On Martin Secker's advice, Mackenzie was reluctantly
surrendering the scheme of a South Seas paradise for the
more practical plan of leasing the Channel Island of Herm.
Lawrence, unaware that his dream was dissolving before it
had formed, was preparing himself for "the reality" by reading Gauguin's *Noa Noa* (later Gauguin was to influence his
style in painting) and Frederick O'Brien's *White Shadows in the
South Seas* ("best thing I've read of late years travels").

By mid-July, the hot sun of the Sicilian summer began to
beat down mercilessly on their heads. Frieda was longing for
her mother and the cool scents of the Black Forest. She
would go to her family alone (it was rumored Germany was
still inhospitable to foreigners), while Lawrence would move
around the familiar haunts of northern Italy, "seeing one
person and another." Both of them would return to Sicily in
October.

Together they took the coastal train north, pausing briefly
in Naples and relaxing for a few days in Amalfi, where they
had friends. Then they went over the mountains to Anticoli-

Corrado (now Fiuggi), the resort reputed to be the home of artists' models, not far from Picinisco and Cassino. Apparently Jan Juta met them there and all three stayed at a farmhouse called San Filipo, "mainly picking flowers."*

In town they met Eric Gill, a "fat-hipped artist" who had been commissioned to paint a portrait of Lady Ottoline Morrell. Some years later, he subscribed to copies of *Lady Chatterly*. Perhaps because Gill was slow in paying for them, Lawrence demolished his *Art Nonsense and Other Essays* when he reviewed it in 1930—the last piece of writing he was able to complete before his death.

The Lawrences spent two weeks in Anticoli and for the next five days wound their way up through Palestrina and Rome to Milan. There they apparently separated,† she continuing up to Germany, Lawrence "wandering around Lake Como and Venice." At Como, he stayed in Argegno, and went on excursions into the hills and on the picturesque island of Comacina. In particular, he enjoyed the atmosphere of a little pastry shop run by an English couple, just opposite the quay. In Venice, he again met Jan Juta, who was there for the exhibition of modern painters at the Biennale d'Arte. Together they attended the show and Lawrence wrote his impressions of it in "America, Listen to Your Own," published in the December 15, 1920, issue of *New Republic*. Lawrence urged American readers to rediscover the ancient sources of their own art—the Mayan, the Aztec, the Inca, the Amerindian—and to be less concerned with the galleries of Venice. In this article, Lawrence may have spent his inter-

---

*Juta said to me that the holiday took place during the summer of 1924, but Lawrence was in America at that time. He probably meant the summer of 1920, since this was the only time Lawrence seems to have stayed in Anticoli.

†Harry Moore in *The Priest of Love* says that they parted company back in Taormina, each making the entire journey alone, but Juta says they were together in Anticoli and the letters speak of "we" until Milan.

est in a book on Venice that he had been invited to write by the firm of John Lane. Though no such book was undertaken, some of the notable sights of the city left their impress on several poems and some of his fiction. For instance, in *Birds, Beasts and Flowers*, the reference to Daniele Manin in "St. Mark" ("A lion with wings./At least at Venice") must have been suggested by the statue of the Venetian patriot in the Campo Manin, where he stands with the lion of Saint Mark at his feet. The allusion to Carpaccio in the same poem indicates that Lawrence must have seen his painting of the lion in the Palazzo Ducale in Venice. The algae-covered canals become the "fucus-dark, seaweed-fringed valleys of the waters . . ." in "St. Matthew." He learned a new term for the Venetian mosquito: "Winged Victory" (in *Birds, Beasts and Flowers*).

Juta was accompanied by his other sister, Luia (later Mrs. Forbes), who was studying singing. According to Juta, Lawrence found her voice so enchanting that he begged her one evening, while the three of them were exploring the canals of the city in a gondola, to sing Brahms *a cappella*. On that occasion, her rendition of Brahms apparently persuaded Lawrence to forget that he had described Venice to his friends as "the stinking, mouldy, oily city of the Doges" afflicted by decrepitude, a touristy place that led him, in the persona of Constance Chatterley, to question the appeal of old Adriatic Italy. Before Lawrence could leave Venice, the English proof of *The Lost Girl* had followed him there and Juta says that he saw Lawrence take the original manuscript, after he had read the proofs, and destroy it page by page.

In early September, he came down to Florence and stayed for a while in a "rambling old explosion shattered villa" in the hills above the city. Rosalind Popham Baynes, who had suggested the farmhouse at Picinisco in the Abruzzi, had rented this dwelling for herself, but when an explosion at a nearby ammunition dump blew out the windows, she moved up to Fiesole and offered Lawrence the windowless villa. Lawrence this time didn't like the atmosphere in his favorite northern city: Florence was in a "state of continual socialistic riot: sudden shots, sudden stones smashing into the restaurants where one was drinking coffee, all the shops suddenly barred and closed."

For most of that month, Lawrence walked the Tuscan hills, prowled about the Etruscan museum in Fiesole (itself of Etruscan origin), called on Leo Stein at the nearby village of Settignano (where he saw his first pictures of Taos), and sometimes took tea or dinner with Rosalind Baynes on the terrace of her villa, gazing down on the gorgeous scene below. Down at the shattered Villa Canovaia, Lawrence was able to compose five of his most magnificent poems in *Birds, Beasts and Flowers*, rough out the six "Tortoise" poems, and conceive the final scenes of violence in *Aaron's Rod*—all bearing the distinct imprint of his experience there.

This creative spurt must have been his main relief from loneliness at the windowless villa (his sole company was the family of the gardener), and toward the end of the month, Lawrence moved to smaller but more comfortable quarters at 35 Viale Milton, not far from Reggie Turner's apartment. Turner had just gotten back from Capri (where was Douglas? "Away with his *amico*"), and before long, Lawrence resumed the pattern of his first stay in Florence—walking the Lungarno, visiting the great galleries, and chatting with friends at their apartments or his own, the while accreting the details for *Aaron's Rod* and possibly for parts of *Lady Chatterley*. On his last day in Florence (October 1), he had tea at Pasakowski's in the company of Reggie Turner and a "charming American widow, a Mrs. Thrasher," who offered him a farm to live on in America (Lawrence brought out the mother in both men and women). The offer interested Lawrence, since he had just received a letter from Mackenzie more or less announcing the end of their mutual dream to hide away in the South Pacific. The letter may have chilled Lawrence's friendship for Mackenzie:

> What is this I hear about Channel Isles?
> The Lord of the Isles.
> I shall write a skit on you one day.
> There will be a lady of the lake in it,
> and a rare to do between the pair.

The seed for "The Man Who Loved Islands" had to be saved for a later time. On the following day, Lawrence had to leave for Venice again, where he was to meet Frieda. Tired of touring and tourists alike, Lawrence was in no mood for a city that demands, for proper appreciation of its delights, strong legs and an unflagging will. On October 7, he writes to Mackenzie again:

> I can't do anything in Venice. Italy feels awfully
> shakey and nasty, and for the first time my un-
> conscious is uneasy of the Italians.

Whether Frieda's arrival caused the gloom to lift must remain unknown, but reunited, the Lawrences stopped briefly in Florence and Rome, caught the steamer from Naples to Sorrento, then the train to Amalfi, where they stayed for several days at the Cappucini Convento, a "charming old monastery." The train to Taormina was delayed for five hours in Messina. Lawrence was profoundly distressed by the signs of the destruction still visible from the earthquake of 1900 and he writes in *Sea and Sardinia*: "I always dread coming near the awful place, yet I have found the people kind, almost feverishly so, as if they know the awful need for kindness." By the evening of October 20 (1920), they had "dribbled their way back to their sanctuary in Sicily."

Hardly had Lawrence unwound from his wandering than he received a note from Don Bernardo at Monte Cassino, asking if he knew that Maurice Magnus had committed suicide in Malta. Lawrence had hoped that Magnus was safely out of his life and that he could forget about him, but the ghost of this "little loving vampire" was already walking toward Sicily, destined to dog Lawrence on and off until 1926. There soon followed an obituary notice from a "scrubby Maltese newspaper" and a long letter of clarification, both posted by a local businessman named Salonia, who had stood surety for Magnus and who had befriended Lawrence during his visit to Malta.

Apparently Magnus, Salonia, and his partner Gabriel Mazzaiba, with whom he owned a business on the wharf, had planned to exploit the commercial possibilities in Morocco. When the scheme fell through for lack of funds and when Salonia learned that Magnus was living beyond his means, he withdrew his guarantee of Magnus's credit, thus making Magnus a potential burden on the inhabitants of Malta. In November, two detectives approached him. Guessing correctly that extradition awaited him, Magnus locked them out of his house, dropped a letter to Don Bernardo out of his window, got into bed, and swallowed a massive dose of prussic acid. Magnus had left a document on his writing table, a kind of cryptic last will. In it he requested a "first class" burial (which he didn't get until his remains were removed from the public cemetery by his loyal friend Mazzaiba and buried in his own, the Mazzaiba grave) and he appointed Norman Douglas as his literary executor (his creditors refused to yield the Foreign Legion manuscript to Douglas and instead asked Lawrence to prepare it for publication).

When Lawrence read this letter from Salonia, he thought: ". . . the world seemed to stand still for me. I knew that in my own soul I had said, 'Yes, he must die if he cannot find his own way.' But for all that, now I *realized* what it must have meant to be the hunted, desperate man: everything seemed to stand still. I could, by giving half my money, have saved his life. I had not chosen to save his life." On later reflection, Lawrence added: "I keep to my choice. I still would not have saved his life. I respect him for dying when he was cornered. And for this reason, I feel still connected with him: still have this to discharge, to get his book published, and to give him his place, to present him just as he was as far as I knew myself." The pressure of other work, either in process or promised, kept Lawrence from taking up the task for more than a year, and consequently, the *Memoirs of the Foreign Legion* was not to appear until 1924, when its publication led to an acrimonious public controversy between Lawrence and Douglas.

Along with his depression over the suicide of Magnus, the unpredictable elements, and the all too predictable protocol of Taormina turned the latter part of 1920 into a winter of discontent. On November 16, he is crotchety to Rosalind Popham Baynes: "It rains with such persistency and stupidity here that one loses all one's initiative and remains cut off . . . Sicily at the moment feels like a land inside an aquarium—all water—and people like crabs and black-grey shrimps creeping on the bottom." A week later he complains to Mary Cannan: "Here we are like marooned sailors . . . these last two days great guns of wind, slashing masses of rain, impossible to open the doors almost. The Taorminisi natives are as mean and creeping as ever. I really begin to feel like you, that one must have done with Italy." The Scandinavians "poking about" bothered him more than the natives.

As the weather brightened up in December, a neighbor named Robert Kitson "popped" the Lawrences into the midst of the social life of the European colony. Though Lawrence gritted that people made him "squeal with impatience," the couple were soon receiving a variety of guests for tea and chocolate cakes (baked by Lawrence): Kitson and an anonymous Frenchwoman; Mrs. Leander Williams, a "withered darling of the Queen Alexandra days"; Jan Juta and Alan Insole; Rosalie Bull, a "rather nice and comic theosophist"; and Alexander Nelson-Hood (the "Duca"). The Francis Brett Youngs came for Christmas, and the Lawrences visited Miss Wallace, the Bouduins, and the young Baron Stempel, whose hobby was taking nude photographs and whom Lawrence liked best of all the Europeans there.

Work was unexciting. He read the first proofs of *Women in Love* and the final proofs of *The Lost Girl* and *Movements in European History* and said that he was "swotting Italian history" because Oxford Press had asked for another chapter on Italian unification. *Aaron's Rod* advanced at a snail's pace and the letters of this period lack luster. Lawrence had struck one of those dreaded creative calms familiar to most artists. Despite the summer of wandering, he felt that he "must dash away" again, before the "terrible dynamic exhalations" of Etna made him mad. In a more restrained vein, he wrote to Mary Cannan that he was "cogitating whether to take this house for another year, or whether to retire to the wilds of Sardinia." He had promised John Lane a book on Venice or Sardinia, but Venice had proved to be impossible and thus all auguries pointed toward Sardinia.

Why Sardinia, "which is like nowhere"? Lawrence writes:

> It lies outside; outside the circuit of civilization. . . . Sure enough, it is Italian now, with its railways and omnibuses. But there is an uncaptured Sardinia still. It lies within the net of this European civilization, and it isn't landed yet.

Lawrence had argued in *Twilight in Italy* and had implied in *The Lost Girl* and *Aaron's Rod* that the English are attracted to the Italians out of a yearning for a purely physical existence. But the real peasant for whom Lawrence was searching eluded him, except in impossibly primitive places like Picinisco. On Sardinia he thought he might penetrate further into the past.

Chapter 6

ON the morning of January 4, 1921, the Lawrences filled a *kitchenino* with provender, packed a knapsack with light gear, closed up their apartment, and started out for Sardinia. They walked through the sleeping town in the cold silence of dawn and descended toward the railway station below, a long steep cobblestone street that still winds down the cliff face to the main highway. In *Sea and Sardinia*, Lawrence remarks:

> Nothing can be more depressing than an Italian high-road. From Syracuse to Airolo it is the same: horrible, dreary, slummy high-roads the moment you approach a village or any human habitation.

By contrast, the majestic grandeur of Etna, the almond blossoms on the steep, and the Ionian Sea provided a thrilling frame for the clerks and other poor workers waiting, like himself, for the early morning train. These Sicilians fascinated Lawrence with their wild exuberance and explosiveness, which he attributed to the influence of Etna: "Never in the world," he writes, "have I seen such melting gay tenderness as between casual Sicilians on railway platforms. . . . They never leave off being amorously friendly with almost everybody, emitting a relentless physical familiarity that is

quite bewildering to one not brought up near a volcano."
After a two-hour journey in the company of "hugely fat
Sicilians with their great macaroni paunches," they reached
Messina. The sight of the "ghostly town," lying shell-
shocked and dripping on the sea "like a broken animal," depressed Lawrence until he glimpsed the characteristic
commotion of the purely Italian scene of the Messina station: the officials "like bees around a hive, humming in an
important *conversazione*. . . . to an Italian official, life seems to
be one long and animated conversation—the Italian word is
better—interrupted by casual trains and telephones." He
notes that a stationmaster in a gold-laced cap walks with a
"little mad hop, and his fingers fly as if he wanted to scatter
them to the four winds of heaven, and his words go off like
fireworks." The passengers huddle together dumbly as the
rain drips off them. Two convicts headed for the Lipari
Islands prison remind him of Oscar Wilde at Reading plat-
form. A pair of large station dogs "run about and trot
through the standing trains, just like the officials. They
climb up the footboard, hop into a train, and hop out casually
when they feel like it."

In Palermo, the Lawrences admired the lobsters, sausage,
and the "fresh delicate flesh of luminous vegetables" piled up
in the marketplace, and window-shopped along the fashionable Via Maqueda. Frieda was put into a towering rage by
"three hussies" who giggled at the incongruous size of Lawrence's knapsack. Lawrence dismissed them with a remark
about bad manners, throwing a nonchalant *"ignoranti,"* but
Frieda was not amused. She chased them off with "strokes
of her sledgehammer Italian," then turned on Lawrence:
"They've followed us the whole length of the street—with
their *sacco militare* and their *parlo inglese* and their *you spik Ingleesh,*
and their jeering insolence. But the English are fools. They
always put up with this Italian impudence." When they
asked a passerby for directions to the Hotel Pantechnico, he

took Lawrence by the hand as though he were "a bit of an imbecile, poor dear," and showed him the way. As refuge from the small traumas of traveling, they spent the evening talking and drinking tea in the room of a young American friend* staying at the same hotel.

In the bleak dawn of the next day, the Lawrences boarded *The City of Trieste*, a "long, slender old steamer with one funnel," bound for Cagliari. Their American friend, who had come to see them off, tried to dissuade them from embarking: their second-class quarters were terribly cramped (the stateroom cost them about twenty-five dollars: the *molto vento* was making rough seas and delaying departure; a rough passage of thirty hours lay ahead. Why didn't they take the short hop from Civitavecchia? But Lawrence was determined to escape and he was already observing the Sardinian passengers with satisfaction when the ship cleared the harbor late that morning and headed for open seas.

The sight of Mount Eryx, the mythical home of the aboriginal Venus, had an unaccountable effect upon him:

> It seems to me from the darkest recesses of my blood comes a terrible echo at the name of Mount Eryx. The name of Athens hardly moves me. At Eryx—my darkness quivers. Eryx, looking west into Africa's sunset. *Erycina ridens.*

The ship called at Trapani, in western Sicily, and since the "Rip van Winkle city" looked as inviting as Mount Eryx, the Lawrences went ashore. The reality was disillusioning: the main avenue which seemed so beautiful from the sea was a

---

*According to Jan Juta, it must have been Elizabeth Humes, who lived in Vienna. However, on January 14, 1921, almost immediately after his return from Sardinia, Lawrence asks Secker to send a copy of *The Lost Girl* to Miss Ruth Wheelock, in the American consulate at Palermo. She might be the American friend referred to.

humpy road littered with rubbish; the disconsolate shops seemed to be selling only rabbit skins and cat skins. And the spread of Socialism was spoiling the inhabitants: ". . . that hateful, unmanly insolence of these lords of toil [a boatman had demanded a larger fee to row them back to their ship], now they have their various 'unions' behind them with their 'rights' as working men, sends my blood black. They are ordinary men no more: the human, happy Italian is most marvelously vanished."

Back aboard, the sight of the Sicilian passengers annoyed Lawrence. One Palermitan family lamented "the cruelties of the journey—and *senza servizio! senza servizio!*" The crew seemed to be no better: ". . . they never do anything but stand in gangs and talk and eat and smoke cigarettes." The ship's carpenter, also a Palermitan, talked incessantly about lire. Lawrence remarks:

> No one can overhear ten words of Italian today without two thousand or two million or ten or twenty or two liras flying like venomous mosquitos round his ears. Liras—liras—liras— nothing else. Romantic, poetic, cypress-and-orange tree Italy is gone.

In the carpenter's voice Lawrence heard all the stridency of postwar Italy. The English and Americans flocked to Italy, with their *sterling* and their *dollari*, and bought what they wanted for nothing, for nothing. *Ecco!* Whereas the poor Italians— "I can't walk a stride," Lawrence comments bitterly, "without having this wretched *cambio*, this exchange, thrown at my head. And this with an injured petulant spitefulness which turns my blood. For I assure them, whatever I have in Italy, I pay for: and I am not England." On another occasion, the carpenter was arguing that Englishwomen were like Neapolitan women in that "underneath they are dirty." Lawrence responded testily, "You who look for dirty women find dirty women everywhere." Surprised, the carpenter assured him that he had misunderstood: "I mean that the Neapolitan women and the English women have dirty underclothing."

The next afternoon the ship arrived at Cagliari and Lawrence managed to get the last bedroom in the Scale di Ferro from the Eskimo-looking owner who at first had offered to give them beds in the *bagno*. The Lawrences spent that day exploring Cagliari. It was carnival time, and at nightfall they enjoyed the spectacle of the masked dancers and other celebrants. Watching the "warm and good-natured" peasants in native dress, Lawrence realized "with horror" that Sardinia was one of the last places in Europe where "the sparks of the old, hardy, indomitable male still survive." Behind those soft, dark eyes, he thought he detected "a stronger, older note: before the soul became self conscious: before the *mentality* of Greece appeared in the world. Remote, always remote, as if the intelligence lay deep within the cave, and never came forward." For the moment, these peasants brought back that "sense of blood familiarity" that he had felt before Mount Eryx, a "nostalgia for something I know not what."

Lawrence yearned for a deeper whiff of "the strange, sinister spirit of place," and on the next afternoon, in the company of a crowd of peasants lugging colorfully woven, "joyful saddle-bags," he and Frieda mounted the train to Mandas, some fifty miles into the interior. As their third-class carriage rattled across the spacious heath, Lawrence succumbed to the "strange magic of Sardinia"—until he observed that most of the peasants working in the fields were clad not in costumes but in leftover military khaki. For him, the ubiquitous cloth symbolized "the universal grey mist that has come over men, the extinguishing of all bright individuality, the blotting out of all wild singleness."

When the train arrived at the little station restaurant in Mandas where they would spend the night, "everyone burst out of the train like seeds from an exploding pod" in search of refreshments. At dinner, the Lawrences were treated to an extraordinary concert of "soup-swilkering" by three local inhabitants:

> The *maialino* was the treble—he trilled his soup into his mouth with a swift sucking vibration, interrupted by bits of cabbage, which made the lamp start to dither again. Black-cap was the baritone; good, rolling spoon-sucks. And the one in spectacles was the bass: he gave sudden deep gulps. All was led by the long trilling of the *maialino*.

The next morning, the Lawrences took the train to Sorgono, a town that lay across the lower slopes of the central range called Gennargentu. The peasants were full of life, shouting and expostulating in their stocking caps, coarse in their individuality, each of them "pivoted and limited to himself, as the wild animals are," untouched by the Christian doctrine of universal love or by the attraction of what is beyond them, knowing how to love their neighbors with "a hot, dark, unquestioning love" only.

Lawrence saw in the Sardinians something unchanging, indomitable, and preworld. They did not cling together, they did not avoid their own individuality, and they had no fear of being alone. Even the Italian spoken on Sardinia Lawrence preferred to the mainland language: it was simple, direct, to the point, more comprehensible. Pride and individuality were symbolized for Lawrence by those long stocking caps the men wore "as part of their inevitable selves." The stocking cap was "a sign of obstinate and powerful tenacity," an indication that the peasants were "not going to be broken in upon the world-consciousness . . . not going into the world's common clothes."

The women, in Lawrence's eyes, were as proud as the men, stones to their flint. They kept "their own backbone stiff and their knuckles hard." There was "something shy and defiant and un-get-at-able" in them that refused to give men too much of their own way. He saw no comradeship between the two, only a fierce sexual battle. There was no happiness, only a fundamental hostility and a destructive passion that reminded him of the clash of the sexes that he had observed in the peasantry of Lake Garda—"the defiant, splendid split between the sexes, each absolutely determined to defend his side, her side from assault." Thus, the encounter between male and female had "a certain wild, salty savour . . . after so much . . . backboneless Madonna-worship . . . and the macaroni slithery-slobbery mess of modern adoration." Like Lilly in *Aaron's Rod*, Lawrence commended "separation and sharp distinction," the counter tide to an ebbing era of love and oneness.

That evening, a bus driver gave a grim but instructive picture of life among the peasants. The islanders were migrating to France and to Rome, the war had practically wiped out the island's cattle, and the arable land was going fallow because the owners refused to spend money on it. Anyway, the peasants hated the land and would do anything rather than work it. They wanted regular wages, shorter hours, and life in the cities. Lawrence and Frieda politely declined an invitation to visit the villages of Abbasanta and Tonara and were glad to catch the morning bus for Nuoro, the former home of Grazia Deledda.*

Outside of Tonara, they watched a procession of villagers chanting antiphonal hymns in honor of the feast of Saint

---

*The Italian novelist who was to win the Nobel Prize for Literature.

Anthony, an occasion that Lawrence turned into one of the best set pieces of *Sea and Sardinia*.

At Nuoro, they witnessed the same feast from the balcony of their room in The Star of Italy. While awaiting dinner, they had to get into bed to be warm. Finally, they were served a meager meal of *bistecca*, potatoes, and cauliflower. The next day (January 10), after promising their friendly bus driver that they would return when the weather was warmer, they left by another bus for Terranova. That evening, they were aboard the small steamer taking them away from Sardinia.

Just as the ancient Etruscan civilization had once faced assimilation into the Roman Empire, so Sardinia stood at the crossroads of conformity and nonconformity. Though Lawrence hoped that his lovely primitive peasants could retain their "vivid clan" distinctions and their "splendid, animal-like stupidity," on his way back home he expressed the fear that the "grey proletarian homogeneity" had already crossed over to Sardinia. The Italy of the intensely individual living spirit was being "smothered by the filthy smother of innumerable lira notes." The cash nexus was stirring up the Sardinians and instilling in their new generation a powerful desire to abandon their island, usually for America or for England. Lawrence, who had encountered peasants caught in similar straits at Lake Garda and Fiascherino, understood the dilemma of the impoverished Sardinians and sympathized with them: uprooting, whatever the cause, made people into exiles, trying painfully to grow a different skin. The Sardinians might succeed in resisting the octopus of "American empire" and surviving as themselves if they would "clothe themselves fiercely for distinction, savage distinction against the rest of the creeping world." It was stocking caps against "khaki all-alikeness." Lawrence makes a similar observation in *Aaron's Rod*, soon after Aaron arrives in postwar Novara.

The book that was born from this brief experience, *Sea and Sardinia*, is no ordinary travelogue: multilayered in its perceptions, it is a genuine "journey into the interior." Though itinerary is stronger than ideology, nevertheless the very complexity of Lawrence's response to dispossessed humanity, the tensions between tempting myths and critical honesty, between the appeal of a fierce, resistant way of life on one hand and the recognition that only a political revolution could change the poverty to which the Sardinian was doomed, make the book an invaluable picture of period Sardinia and a revealing mirror of Lawrence's preoccupations of that time.

By the next morning, the ship deposited its passengers at Civitavecchia, an old medieval-looking port that Lawrence would revisit during his Etruscan pilgrimage. On the train headed south, once more reading *Corriere della Sera*, Lawrence felt his Sardinian soul melting off him, felt himself "evaporating into the real Italian uncertainty and Momentaniety." In Rome (January 11, 1921) before changing trains for Naples, Lawrence and Frieda met Alan Insole and Jan Juta. A hurried "four-branched candlestick of a conversation" took place, during which Juta proposed that Lawrence return to Sardinia with him the coming May so that they could collaborate on a book, Lawrence "doing the scribbling and he the pictures." Lawrence agreed to the collaboration. *Sea and Sardinia* was the result, but the proposed trip did not take place.*

Once more the Lawrences rolled south on the train, past the great abbey of Monte Cassino perched on its hill. In a wild moment, Lawrence suggested that they spend the night

---

*During the summer of 1921, Juta brought the illustrations to Florence for approval. Lawrence drew a map of the island (printed in the first edition) and sent the typescript and illustrations to Seltzer, who published the book. The original manuscript, according to Frieda, ended up in the WC of Fontana Vecchia.

there and "see the other friend, the monk who knows so much about the world, being out of it (he probably meant Don Bernardo), but Frieda merely shuddered at the prospect of "the awful winter coldness of that massive stone monastery." Lawrence had to be content with coffee and sweet cakes at the Cassino station.

The remainder of the ride was enlivened by a compartment full of D'Annunzio's soldiers returning from the fiasco at Fiume. As though exorcising the defeat of their leader, they defiantly sang the bragging songs of the legion until silenced by a regular-army officer and their own "sheer dispirited fatigue." When the train arrived at the "vast and thievish" station in Naples, Lawrence saw that the coach going to Syracuse was too crowded and decided to chance *The City of Trieste*, departing that night for Palermo. With knapsack over his shoulder and with *kitchenino* in Frieda's hand, the two of them "plunged through the black wet gulf of a Naples night" toward the port. At the ticket window, with one hand on his wallet (he still remembered the two times he had been robbed in Italy) and the other warding off the competition, Lawrence somehow struggled through the mob and procured tickets for two cabins, which turned out to be "palatial."

Soon they were at sea, and as the ship passed Anacapri, Lawrence "sent out a few thoughts to a few people on the island." The following morning, when the rocky coast of Sicily hove into view, Lawrence felt a bit like Ulysses "stealing into these magic harbours." After the ship docked, he was so glad to be on his own feet that he walked the longish distance with Frieda to the Hotel Panoramus.

That evening, once more in the company of the American girl, they went to a puppet theater on a back street in Palermo. His description of the performance, on the final pages of *Sea and Sardinia*, should be placed alongside the chapter called "The Theatre" in *Twilight in Italy* and his essay on a people's theater.* Lawrence was charmed by the brilliant, human-sized marionettes who enacted, with "sudden, angular gestures" the story of Orlando and the paladins of France.

When the performance was over, Lawrence shook hands with his neighbor in the next seat, "affectionately, and in the right spirit," and sighed to himself, "Truly I love them all in the theatre: the generous, hot southern blood, so subtle and spontaneous, that asks for blood contact, not for mental communion or spirit sympathy." It was probably in such a mood that Lawrence arrived back at the Fontana Vecchia on January 13 of 1921.

A week later, he wrote to Eleanor Farjeon, the author and sister of the playwright Herbert Farjeon, that he had liked Sardinia very much, that its people had converted him into a "revolutionary socialist" (c.f. his railing against the Sicilian Socialists in "Hibiscus and Salvia Flowers"), but confessed that there was "no point in living there," as he once thought he might. It was, finally, "a stray corner of Italy, rather difficult materially to live in." And Sicily? In the midst of hailstorms and "deadly cold weather," it was losing its old dark magic. After the north, the south of Italy seemed lifeless: ". . . I really don't believe I shall come back for another winter." An early spring turned frigid Taormina "green and flowery," and soon Lawrence was assuring Koteliansky that he once more "loved his Fontana Vecchia." The wintery images and the metaphors of rebirth make it likely that "Bare Fig Trees," "Bare Almond Trees," and "Almond Blossoms," that trio of remarkable poems in *Birds, Beasts and Flowers*, belong to this period.

By now, however, Lawrence was itching to leave the island. He thought seriously of going to America and taking the farm that Mrs. Thrasher had offered to him, "4 hours

*It serves as the preface to *Touch and Go*.

from New York, 2 hours from Boston." Possibly he could write for American audiences while working the 90 acres with the help of Vincenzo and Ciccia, his landlord's sister and her husband, who were pining for a new life. For reasons that Lawrence does not make clear, the arrangements fell through (apparently he had hoped to exchange dwellings with Mrs. Thrasher). Disappointed, Lawrence began to weigh Juta's proposal for a walking trip through Sardinia. Juta went but Lawrence did not.

Meanwhile, Frieda had been called to the aid of her ailing mother in Baden-Baden (at first Lawrence suspected that Frieda's sister, Else Jaffe, who had been so sympathetic earlier, was trying to separate them); during the second week of March Lawrence accompanied Frieda to Palermo, saw her aboard ship, spent a weekend at the Panoramus, "where our friend lived," and returned to Taormina. On the following days, he worked hard enough to finish Part I of a novel to be called "Mr. Noon"; a volume of poetry (*Birds, Beasts, and Flowers*); and the book of travel sketches to be known as *Sea and Sardinia*. Neighbors showered him with invitations. Millicent Beveridge, a Scottish painter, came over regularly to paint his portrait ("I look quite a sweet young man"), but Fontana without Frieda echoed with emptiness. After enduring almost a month of loneliness—paradoxically made more acute by the annual arrival of tourists—Lawrence decided to join her in Germany, visiting friends as he wandered up the mainland. On April 9, he caught a ship from Palermo to Capri. Mackenzie was away at his Channel Island of Herm, but Lawrence was made welcome by Earl and Achsah Brewster, an expatriate American couple. Lawrence accepted their invitation to stay at their villa, the Quattro Venti, and immediately slipped into an easy relationship with them, mimicking their mutual acquaintances in Taormina and chatting about his work. The Brewsters, who were preparing to study Buddhism in Ceylon, tried to bring the light of Asia to their new friend, but apparently were unsuccessful.

One afternoon, Lawrence entertained them by recounting the plot of his novel-in-progress, up to the time that Aaron sheds his wife and family. The Brewsters felt that Aaron should have to go to Monte Cassino and repent, or else go through the whole cycle of human experience. This first suggestion amused Lawrence, since he himself had considered the possibility of putting Aaron in the monastery before deciding that his hero "had to go to destruction to find his way from the lowest depth."

Lawrence left the Brewsters on cheerful terms (they were to become firm friends) and broke his trip north by staying overnight in Rome with Ellesina Santoro. On April 21, he arrived in Florence on the slow train "laden with poor folks that could not pay for speed." He took a room in a hotel along the river, probably Birchelli's, the Bertolini's of "A Railway Journey" in *Aaron's Rod*. The following day, as Rebecca West, Norman Douglas, and Reggie Turner were lunching together, it occurred to them, almost simultaneously, that they ought to visit Lawrence and welcome him on behalf of all expatriate Englishmen. Douglas crashed into the room first, and saw Lawrence picking away at a typewriter. Facetiously he asked whether the work in progress dealt with the present state of Florence and Lawrence answered that it did (it may have been the final draft of *Aaron's Rod*). Lawrence put down his work and played host: the three visitors sat alongside one another on the bed, and nodding at appropriate moments, were so captivated by his conversation that they lost their curiosity about what he had been typing. The following day the foursome went walking in the Tuscan hills. As Rebecca West listened to Lawrence's complaints about the discomforts of travel, she concluded that he was like the Indian fakir or the Russian saint who embarked upon journeys with a spiritual rather than geographical destination in mind. "Lawrence travelled, it seemed, to get a certain Apocalyptic vision of mankind," Miss West was to write some years later, "that he registered again and again and again, always rising to a pitch of ecstatic agony."

The next day, Lawrence left Florence (Rebecca West never saw him again) and by the end of April, was reunited with Frieda in Baden-Baden. They spent the summer together in the Black Forest and at Zell am See in the Austrian Tyrol. During this period, Lawrence finished *Aaron's Rod* and edited for the *Dial* Koteliansky's translation of "The Gentleman from San Francisco,"* complimenting his Russian friend for the way that he had skillfully preserved Bunin's "screamingly good" picture of Naples and Capri. He also toyed with the idea of doing a history of Italian painting for children (the book never materialized because Lawrence felt that the illustrations of the Medici Society were not good enough). Frieda, who loved Zell am See, wanted to stay on, and was "quite bitter" when Lawrence, restless again and homesick for Italy, insisted upon leaving. A friend, Nelly Morrison, had offered them her furnished apartment in Florence "for not very much," and Lawrence announced his plans to the Carswells, who were scheduled to visit Zell am See (but didn't):

> If it keeps so hot I shall stay somewhere near
> Meran [Merano] for a while, and perhaps look
> around and see if I might like to live there. I
> don't much want to go back to Taormina again.
> If the weather breaks, and it rains, I shall go to
> Florence.

The weather did break, and the Lawrences descended lei-

---

*Lawrence is called a "collaborator" in the first American edition, but clearly his knowledge of Russian hardly warranted such an honor.

surely through Merano, Bolzano, Cortina, and Bologna, arriving in Florence on August 29.

Nelly Morrison's second-floor apartment in the ancient palazzo at 32 Via de' Bardi proved to be redolent of the Renaissance. The arched apertures and the glistening, dark red floors of the "lofty, silent ancient rooms" must have reminded them that George Eliot's Romola dwelt there before becoming a disciple of Savonarola. On one side of the dining room the windows opened onto the narrow street below, and on the other, faced the Uffizi Palace and the lovely old city itself. During the long relaxed afternoons, Lawrence wrote and read. When the wind off the Arno wasn't too strong, the maid served them dinner on the terrace, and in the evenings Lawrence watched the changing of the guard at the Ponte Vecchio or idly traced the flight of bats. Lawrence grew so fond of the apartment that he wrote Nelly Morrison that he intended to write a story about the old house: it became part of the shifting scene in "Things" but the best description of it went into a long poem describing Lawrence's encounter with a bat that had entered but could not escape from his "crash box" of a room over the "great stone rattle" of the Via de' Bardi.

In such easy surroundings, the Lawrences waxed hospitable. Mary Cannan, fresh from France, found their company congenial, and impressed by their apartment, took the one above it in order to be near them (Lawrence, however, was beginning to be bored by her because she insisted on trying to "manage" him). Jan Juta, bearing the illustrations for *Sea and Sardinia*, came several times to consult over the number and the price of the prints for *Sea and Sardinia* (they were done in Germany), and apparently members of the expatriate faithful were frequent callers. But their most valued guests were the Carswells, who had come to Florence for a week's stay. The Lawrence look of that period is preserved for us in Mrs. Carswell's prose: "Owing to the placing of short stories in the United States through Mountsier, Lawrence had become distinctly more prosperous than he had been when I last saw him. This was reflected in his and Frieda's clothes. If he would never be a dandy, he nonetheless liked to appear in the unmistakable role of *il signore*." Once settled into an inexpensive *pensione* not far from Lawrence, Catherine Carswell introduced him to some of her Anglo-Italian cousins (who, she says, definitely did not treat him in a manner befitting a *signore*), and Lawrence introduced her to a number of well-known residents of Florence and to several stray people who whirled for the time in "his orbit." The most notable of the former was a man with a "smallish clean-shaven face that managed to be at once red and dried up" (Reggie Turner?) and the most memorable of the latter was a "large American woman . . . studying singing," whose son was given to the Fascist salute. At the Via de' Bardi, sometimes Lawrence would amuse his friends with his gift of mimicry, specializing in mob scenes, and on another occasion, all four of them, the Carswells and the Lawrences, celebrated his thirty-sixth birthday over dinner, "gay in a quiet sort of way."

Of their daily meetings and good talks together, Lawrence wrote to Catherine Carswell when he returned to Taormina, ". . . it seems only a moment we saw you—but the sympathy is there." She too had felt as drawn as ever to Lawrence, but sensed that despite his geniality, there was something "restless, remote, and even impatient about him," suggesting that for the time being at least he was weary of Europe and Italy.

This restless mood may account for the relatively modest accomplishments of almost a month's sojourn in Florence: he wrote only three poems ("Bat," "Man and Bat," and "Fish") and parts of two stories, and limited his reading to Nelly Morrison's "battered volumes" of Casanova—whom he dismissed as pornographic *crotte*. Late in September, he and Frieda undertook a tour of Siena and Perugia, neither of which they had seen. They planned to meet the Carswells in Siena, and after taking leave of each other, to call at Capri to see the Brewsters. But travel was very "disheartening" that year—"not so much the inconvenience as the kind of slow poison one breathes in every new atmosphere." Perhaps this "poison" working on his perturbed spirit may explain why he loathed Siena, the best-preserved outdoor museum in Italy. Instead of waiting for the Carswells or visiting Perugia ("I'm sick of *gaping* things, even Peruginos," he said in *Sea and Sardinia*), the Lawrences went down to Rome, where "a drive far out on the Campagna" made Lawrence feel better. The train trip from Rome to Naples must have been unusually grueling, for he says it made him ill in Capri. Nevertheless, at the Brewsters' villa, he entertained his hosts by imitating Florence Farr talking Yeats's poems to the psaltery* and enjoyed his stay of five days (September 22–27). On the twentieth-eighth of September, amid "whirlwind and rain," he and Frieda arrived home in Taormina.

Lawrence remained in Sicily for another four and a half months. Tired of travel, he seemed genuinely glad to be home. At moments during this period, the old fires of affection for the south revived—for instance, on the night of *Tutti Morti*, when the local cemetery was "lit up with bundles of light like yellow crocuses" while Carmelo and Grazia lay in wait for the ghost that might steal their paraffin lamps; or when Calabria twinkled "like seven jewels" below; or when the "white trumpet tree under the balcony perfumed six

---

*"Have you ever heard Florence Farr do her ping-wanging . . . Lawrence began chanting monotonously: 'You who are bent and bald and blind.' Paused, then stretched his thin hands over his knees delicately, as if an instrument lay there, plucked an imaginary string and whined, 'Pi . . . . ing . . . wa . . . ng.' Deepening his voice, 'with heavy heart' staccato ping-wang, 'and a wandering mind.' And he ping-wanged . . . violently." From a letter by Earl Brewster.

heavens with sweetness." He tried to persuade Catherine
Carswell that if she were to come to Sicily she would discover why he still liked "this place" best of all.

Yet soon afterward he had to confess to her that "Italy
has for some reason gone a little rancid in my mouth,"
adding that the European colony was turning Taormina into
a "continental Mad Hatter's party—and you wonder who on
earth is going head over heels into the teapot next." The
townspeople were getting under his skin and his English
countrymen didn't like the way he dressed. A strike of the
railroad workers sent food prices up and emptied the antique
shops in Taormina. The critics, including amateurs like
Frieda, mercilessly mistreated *Aaron's Rod*. To Jan Juta he
fumed, "Oh I get so sick of everything; and so double-sick of
Taorminity," and in a letter to Earl Brewster, who had just
reached the tranquillity of Kandy, Lawrence's cup ran over:
" . . . it is a world of canaille: absolutely. *Canaille, canáglia,
Schweinhunderei*, stink-pots. Pfui!—pish, pshaw, prrr! They all
stink in my nostrils." Even nature conspired against him: the
November sirocco bringing "hot billows of wet and clinging
mist" was followed by icy blasts; and a mail train which he
believed might be carrying a manuscript of his fell into a
river at Calabria.

Despite such small disturbances of man and climate, he
worked steadily to complete two projects before leaving
Europe: a volume of short stories (to be entitled *England, My
England*) and a collection of three novellas, each of which he
had written or revised that winter. He pondered the possibility of translating Giovanni Verga—had anyone yet done
him into English? he wanted to know. He found Verga's
work fascinating, even though it made Lawrence, no stranger to the poverty of Italy, "feel quite sick at the end." He
queried Catherine Carswell about the secret of the Etruscans, that mysterious lost people whose funerary sculpture

in the Fiesole and Roman museums had so aroused his curiosity that past summer.

While Lawrence was pondering the past, the *Corriere della Sera* was bringing news about disorders in Rome. The "communisti" and the "fascisti" were fighting each other in the streets, like the Guelphs and the Ghibellines. In these events Lawrence saw portents of a "mild sort of revolution" and the emergence of an industrial-clerical Fascism. He confided to Earl Brewster that he still wanted "a little farm," somewhere in Mexico, New Mexico, the Rocky Mountains, or British Columbia. Therefore, when another generous but strange American woman, Mabel Dodge, offered him a furnished adobe lodge at Taos, New Mexico with real Indians nearby, Lawrence was enticed and excited. Not long before, at Leo Stein's villa near Fiesole, he had seen pictures of Taos and perhaps some of the paintings of the artists who lived there. And Stein told him that New Mexico was the most fantastic place on earth. He had long been fascinated by Aztec culture and the Amerinds, and he noticed that the word "Taos" was a bit like "Taormina"—a good omen. But in January, while still weighing the prospect, he came down with the flu, which lasted for three weeks. The illness, he thought, was "the blood and psyche" telling him that he was at the end of his "particular tether in Europe."

Though he continued to talk about what fun it would be to take that adobe lodge in New Mexico, he must have sensed that in his weakened condition it would be unwise to cross the cold North Atlantic to an American winter. Thus, as he was about to book passage to America, it came over him that America at the moment was "too raw" for him and he "too tender" for it and that he must first go to Ceylon—a perfect detour since Brewster, who was studying Pali and Buddhism at a monastery, had just offered the Lawrences the use of a "big ramshackle" bungalow in Kandy. To his

agent Curtis Brown, he wrote: "I shall go with my wife
there, for a bit. Wish me God-speed (not into the monastery)." A year in the Far East, where he could experience the
reality of the inner world firsthand, might "sweeten the gall
in his blood" and prepare him for his great onslaught on
Western civilization.

On February 20, Lawrence and Frieda left for Ceylon. En
route to the ship they stopped in Palermo at the Hotel Panoramus, and on the next day, took the steamer to Naples. The
next three days they spent at the Hotel Santa Lucia on the
waterfront, resavoring the city and its setting. When the
weather was clear, Capri sparkled invitingly across the bay,
but they were set for Ceylon. On February 26, they boarded
the S. S. *Osterley*, carrying baskets of fruit brought by Capri
friends and "a piece of Sicilian wagon painted very gaily with
two scenes out of the life of Marco Visconte."* As they
climbed up the gangplank, the porters cried out: "*Ecco la
Sicilia—Ecco la Sicilia in viaggio per l'India!*" ("Look here at
Sicily—Look at Sicily on the way to India!"). At eight o'clock
in the evening, the *Osterley* cleared the harbor and Frieda
went to bed immediately with a cold that she had caught in
Naples. On the next morning, as they steamed through the
Strait of Messina, Lawrence saw Etna "like a white queen or
a white witch standing there in the sky," saying to him,
"'You come back here.'" Lawrence "wept inside with grief,
grief of separation." He and Frieda had spent two reasonably
happy years in its shadow.†

On the voyage through the Suez Canal and halfway
across the Indian Ocean, Lawrence worked on his translations of Verga. In his introduction to *Mastro Don Gesualdo*, he

---

*Lawrence may have meant Matteo Visconti, the thirteenth-century
statesman who opposed the Della Torre family in Milan. Lawrence used
the Della Torre name in *Aaron's Rod*.

†The plaque on the south wall of Fontana Vecchia gives the dates incor-
rectly as 1920–1923.

contends that *Cavalleria Rusticana* contains some of the best short stories ever written. In May of 1923, he writes to Murry from Mexico, offering to let him publish either "Cavalleria Rusticana" or "La Lupa" in the *Adelphi*. None of the nine stories of *Cavalleria* appeared in the magazine, although several of the *Little Novels* did.

The translations are splendid accomplishments, to which Lawrence brought all his sensibilities, capturing as nearly as he could in English prose the idiom of the original, effacing his own style and personality in order to advance the author's.* At the outset, each story gives a sense of the jumble and the incoherence, "the breathless muddle of the peasant mind," Lawrence wrote. Once the narration is under way, the manner is concise, swift, and lyrically simple. Verga's technique is "to follow the workings of the unsophisticated mind, and . . . to reproduce the pattern." Even in the unorthodox punctuation, Verga is "aiming at the same muddled swift effect of the emotional mind in its movements . . . The emotional mind, however apparently muddled, has its own rhythm, its own commas and colons and full-stops."

Certain important qualities of Verga's style may have influenced the later stories of Lawrence, especially those in which the earlier lushness and lyricism of style give way to a more flexible prose that accommodates itself to more varieties of experience.

In early 1922, Lawrence wrote an essay designed to serve as a preface to *Don Gesualdo*. It was rejected in favor of a shorter piece. In the rejected introduction, a beautiful blend of penetrating criticism and personal experience, Lawrence reveals familiarity with the work of Manzoni, Deledda, Pirandello, and D'Annunzio, but clearly Verga is his favorite.

---

*For a careful study, see Robert Henderson's "D. H. Lawrence as a Translator of Italian," a University of Texas dissertation.

He writes: "Perhaps the deepest nostalgia I have ever felt has been for Sicily, reading Verga. Not for England or anywhere else—for Sicily, the beautiful, that which goes deepest into the blood."

It was sometime late in March that they settled into their bungalow on a lake near Kandy. Lawrence could endure the steaming heat for only a month (he feared the ultraviolet rays from the sun would decompose his blood). Also, he couldn't stand the "bottomless, hopeless eyes" of the naked natives and he hated their Buddha, with "his rat-hole temples and his rat-hole religion." From Ceylon, the Lawrences went to Australia and by June 1 were installed in a bungalow near Sydney, which he jokingly called "Wyewurk." Almost immediately he wrote to a friend announcing "a bitter burning nostalgia for Europe and for Sicily." The Lawrences remained there for a period of four months, and on August 10, 1922, sailed for America.

PART III

Italy Lost and Found

(September 1922–July 1929)

Chapter 7

READING *Sea and Sardinia*, Mabel Dodge was overpowered by Lawrence's vivid impressions of that primitive place. "I wanted him to know Taos," she says, "before it became exploited and spoiled."

America had a dual attraction for Lawrence: the challenge of the newest in Western civilization, and the fascination of its aboriginals who had survived these surroundings. The Lawrences sailed for San Francisco, stopped at New Zealand, Rarotonga, and Tahiti. The South Sea Islands were a disappointment and led Lawrence to conclude: "So far I like Taormina as well as anything I have seen: we may go back there."

They reached New Mexico in September of 1922. During that winter, Lawrence seemed content at the nearby Del Monte ranch, but when he learned that Mary Cannan was going to Venice and Lucca, he wrote plaintively: "Tell me what Italy is like now. My heart still turns most readily to Italy." However, he was not yet ready to return, and after six months in the Southwest, he moved down to Chapala in Mexico. Among the inhabitants there the pure-blooded Indians interested him the most, probably because he saw in them something that reminded him of the "dark blood consciousness" that he had found fascinating in the Italian peasant. Toward the fall of 1923, while Frieda was in Europe, he visited Los Angeles and then went back to Guadalajara, Mexico.

In November, he left Mexico for England and early in

December 1923 was reunited with Frieda in London. After
visits to Paris and Baden-Baden, they returned to the United
States in March 1924 and after arriving in Taos, they took
up quarters on a run-down ranch, which Mabel Dodge had
given Frieda in exchange for the holograph manuscript of
Sons and Lovers with David Garnett's corrections on it. The
ranch was known as the Lobo and later as the Kiowa.

Most of that fall and winter was spent in Mexico, mainly
in Oaxaca. Despite the serene climate and a "dark, dangerous
quality" about the region, Lawrence writes to Earl Brewster
in December 1924: "I have a bit of longing for Italy. . . .
Perhaps in the spring we will sail to Naples; and perhaps
then we can walk in Calabria or the Abruzzi" (instead they
were to tour the Etruscan cities together). During this
period, Lawrence wrote *Mornings in Mexico* and finished his
Mexican novel, *The Plumed Serpent.* Here he experimented
further with the idea of "blood consciousness" (which, to put
it briefly, becomes phallic power).* But the pure primitive in
the end did not satisfy Lawrence's intelligence. The Mexican
peasants whom Cipriano and Ramon command seem at first
to be New World developments of the peasants Lawrence
knew in Italy. But this is not quite true. There is a difference.
Held down by the tangle of sun and earth, the Mexican
peasants are subject to a demonic hatred of life itself. This is
precisely opposite to the feelings that Lawrence sensed were
down deep in the Italian. ·The Italian also suffered from a
soul strangled by the past, but there remained nonetheless a
genial, tender quality about his life. The vital Etruscan effu-

---

*During the thirties and forties, Lawrence's sinister dark gods and
horny heroes gave the book an undeservedly bad name. Many critics saw
a resemblance to the Nazi worship of hero cults and pagan gods. However, Lawrence had in mind an ideal, born in the Mediterranean, which
somehow went wrong in Mexican dress. This ideal was of the priest-
king, the specially gifted, initiated being, similar to the Etruscan Lucomo
or the aristocratic little Count Dionys in the short novel, *The Ladybird*,
who could draw the vital forces of the cosmos into himself, a life bringer
to his people and a guide to the mysteries beyond life.

sion, though underground, was still there, surviving among the peasants living in quiet corners of Italy that still resisted modern industrial civilization. His Mexican essays reveal his awareness of a gulf between Western consciousness and that of the true primitive: "I don't want to live again the tribal mysteries my blood has lived long since." Lawrence was seeking a balance, an integration of all forces that appeared opposite—mind and instinct, male and female, sensate and insensate. As he was to say in his introduction to *New Poems*, "Life is so made that opposites sway about a trembling centre of balance." But he invested enormous energy in the final exploration of the possibilities of the unconscious and instinctual forces in our lives. Perhaps he spent too much in this creative effort. He fell seriously ill from an attack of malaria (which he may have picked up in Ceylon). At the beginning of April 1925, while recuperating at their little ranch, he learned that Norman Douglas had attacked him over the publication of Magnus's *Memoirs*.

According to Richard Aldington, Douglas had been angered, understandably, by the caricature of himself as Argyle* in *Aaron's Rod* and therefore was not in the least reluctant to vilify Lawrence at the bidding of a "rich woman who bore a grudge" against him. In a privately printed pamphlet signed "N.D.," Douglas charged that Lawrence had deeply wronged Magnus and had personally profited from the publication of his *Memoirs*, taking money that should have been his. He mocked what he regarded as Lawrence's mean-spirited concern with money and his bourgeois standards for judging the actions of Magnus.

Lawrence responded to the attack by publishing in *The New Statesman* a letter that Douglas had written to him, which read in part: "By all means do what you like with the MS. As to M. Himself, I may do some kind of memoir of him later on—independent of foreign legions. Put me into your intro-

---

*In a letter to Martin Secker (November 23, 1921) Lawrence writes: "Do you think Douglas will identify himself with Argyle and be offended? I think not." Lawrence says that he meant no resemblance.

duction, if you like—*Pocket all the cash yourself.*" Privately, Lawrence told Curtis Brown that the only reason he had bothered about the manuscript was that Magnus owed Gabriel Mazzaiba fifty-five pounds and Salonia ten pounds. When Seltzer, his American publisher, had offered to bring out the introduction under a separate imprint, he had refused and had waited for the chance to have the entire manuscript accepted. Furthermore, before turning the manuscript over to an English publisher, he had taken the trouble to authenticate it to his own satisfaction by going over it carefully with Magnus himself.

Jan Juta, who had first brought the manuscript to Lawrence's attention, and who was horrified by the Douglas diatribe, said that Lawrence had written the introduction for the sake of Magnus's memory rather than for the hope of profit.*

Is it possible that the feud with Douglas stirred a longing for Italy? In the summer of 1925, Lawrence is saying to Frieda, "The Mediterranean is glittering blue again," and at dinner once, he comments, "There is no fish as good as in Italy." To Dorothy Brett, he remarks, "Everyone who can ought to see Italy. I am to be there this winter. Why don't you go to Capri?"†

In November of 1925, after enduring a week in New York

---

*Lawrence asked for and apparently got only ten percent on the sale of the first 2000 copies by Secker.

†Dorothy Brett was the daughter of the Viscount Esher. She was a deaf and shy painter totally devoted to Lawrence, whom she met during World War I. When she learned the Lawrences were leaving England she threw a farewell party for them which turned into a drunken disaster. She was present with his other friends at the famous "Last Supper" at the Café Royal when Lawrence invited them all to join him in founding a colony on the slopes of the Rockies. All but Brett were evasive—she went to New Mexico with the Lawrences. Mabel Dodge called her the "holy Russian idiot" because she followed Lawrence around on the ranch, her ear trumpet protruding.

City, the Lawrences left America for good and returned temporarily to England, hoping to end their slow, fitful journey around the world. Using London as a base, they visited friends and family: a trip to Eastwood to see Lawrence's sister ("the weather's awful, and we simply hate it up here") and to High Wycombe to see the Carswells. Despite warm welcome everywhere, homecoming was dreary. From Baden-Baden, old Baroness Richthofen beckoned, but two weeks there was enough: it was "unbelievably quiet and deserted . . . nothing but ghosts, from the Turgenev period." As before when England and the gray north had proved depressing, Lawrence decided to seek the sun of Italy for the winter ("either try Italy and the sun, or a Devonshire village," Lawrence had recently written to an aspiring young writer whose "visionary *soul*" needed "thawing out"). They came through Lucerne to Milan and once more followed "the old, old imperial road" that had taken them south to Genoa before.

This time Lawrence wanted to try the western Riviera again, but by coincidence, Martin Secker was in Spotorno, not far from Monte Carlo, with his Italian wife Rina. Lawrence came to Spotorno to see his English publisher, and when he learned that very few tourists stopped at this fishing village, he decided that it would be a better place than the western Riviera for the winter. Secker took a room for him at the Villa Maria, a small inn run by the family Capellero, and by November 16, Lawrence is informing Curtis Brown: "It is a pleasant, sunny day, with a dark blue sea, and I sit writing outside on the balcony just above the beach" (he may have been referring to *The Virgin and the Gipsy,* a story about two girls who return to England from Lucerne, where Lawrence himself had stayed just two weeks earlier).

The next day Frieda saw, near the ruins of a castle, "a pink villa that had a friendly look." On wandering up to the place, they met a peasant named Giovanni, whom they asked about renting it. Yes, he must have said, it belonged to the wife of a "tenente de' bersagliere," Angelo Ravagli, who lived in Savona. The peasant then took charge. When the *tenente* arrived at the Villa Maria, Lawrence went out to negotiate with him and returned shortly to Frieda: "You can come—and a man so pleasant and witty." Since there was a military parade that day, Angelo Ravagli was wearing his best uniform, "with gay plumes and a blue sash." They went to the Villa Bernardo together and the conditions for renting were arranged, twenty-five pounds sterling for five months— until April 15.

On the Feast of Saint Catherine (November 25), while the men of the village were "all sitting around the little tables, down below, drinking wine or vermouth," Lawrence completed the final chapter of *Mornings in Mexico*, called "Some Moonshine with Lemon." This passage is the most nostalgic that Lawrence ever wrote about his "little ranch" in America. Indeed it was nostalgia, brought on by the vermouth and the "broad white shimmer" of the Mediterranean moon that reminded him of silvery New Mexico nights. But this sentimental longing for his "three horses down among the timber," Susan, his black cow, and *"un poco di chiar' di luna, con canella [sic] e limone"* ("a little moonshine with cinnamon and lemon"), was gradually dispelled by the sound of Giovanni's voice fondly calling out, *"Valo gui, Signore Lorenzo! Buona notte!"* the whispering of the Mediterranean, "so eternally young," and perhaps a wave of appreciation for his new spacious quarters, "nice but blowy." Less than a month later, he was saying to Dorothy Brett: "The thought of the ranch now makes me shudder."

The "three-decker villa" (now called the Pensione Château) had a beautiful garden in the rear, graceful palm trees in front, and a commanding view of the Mediterranean Sea. Lawrence described their new life to his mother-in-law:

> Now it is evening: we are sitting in the kitchen
> high under the roof . . . . Underneath, the lights

> of the village lie like oranges and tangerines,
> little and shining. . . . The soup is boiling. In a
> moment we call down into the depths: *Viene,*
> *Giovanni, e pronto il mangiare.* Then the old man
> runs up the stairs like an unhappy frog, with his
> nose in the air, sniffing and smelling. It is nice
> for him to know that there is always something
> good for him to eat.

Christmas of 1925 was celebrated over a turkey dinner at the local inn with Frieda's daughter, Barbara Weekley, the Seckers, and the Capelleros. To a friend he wrote: "It's real Italian country style—a pleasant sort of life, easier than America."

These surroundings proved to be modestly productive. By the end of that year, Lawrence had read proof on his play *David*, and had probably completed the first draft of *The Virgin and the Gipsy* and the final version of four stories: "The Rocking-Horse Winner," "Glad Ghosts," "Sun," (which has a Sicilian setting), and "Smile" (which has a Ligurian setting). He must have written all of them by hand, for he sent the manuscripts over to Capri, where Dorothy Brett typed and returned them. As compensation, Lawrence paid her the going rate, told her about the glories of *strega*, and promised to visit her as soon as he could afford the trip. With almost no tourists to talk to, Lawrence sharpened his command of Italian, and his letters of the period are peppered with passages in Italian. To John Middleton Murry he says:

> *Carino, basta! Carito, deja, deja, la canzon, cheto! Cheto,*
> *cheto! Zitto, zitto, +zitto! Basta la mossa!* In short, shut
> up.

But as the winter wore on, the wind off the snow-capped mountains dropped the temperatures to freezing, and he and Frieda, sometimes joined by the equally uncomfortable Seckers, would huddle in the kitchen with a "warm *stufa*

economica, which is anything but economical." Angelo Ravagli, who was to become Frieda's husband, said that Lawrence looked peaked and ill-tempered much of the time,
perking up only when the sun was warm.* The blustery
winds no doubt bothered him, especially while he was ill, and
made him long for the milder climate of Amalfi, Calabria,
and Sicily or dream about owning a yacht on which he could
sail the coast of the Mediterranean with Earl Brewster, calling at ports such as Constantinople and Damascus [*sic*].
Nevertheless, Lawrence was glad to be back on the Mediterranean again—it seemed, he said, "so versatile and so young,
after America, which is everywhere tense."

Despite the comforting presence of the Seckers, the Lawrences must have felt somewhat lonely and isolated on the
wintry Riviera. Lawrence urged Murry to visit them (he
didn't) and Frieda invited her daughter Barbara for an
extended stay. Shortly afterward, in mid-February, his sister
Ada Lawrence Clarke and her companion, a Mrs. Booth,
arrived in Turin for a two weeks' holiday on the Riviera.
Lawrence went over and fetched them, while Barbara was
being moved to a hotel in Alassio, some thirty kilometers
away, in order to make room for the two Englishwomen. A
few days later, Frieda's older daughter Elsa and a Mrs. Sea-
man† joined Barbara at the "little Hotel Ligure," and
together the sisters would travel over to the Villa Bernardo
to spend a day with their mother and stepfather. Angelo
Ravagli says that whenever the mother and daughters were
reunited, Lawrence would become irritable because he
would feel left out. Furthermore, Ada and Frieda were fed
up with each other and feuding. Before long, Ada persuaded

---

*Ravagli would come over on Sundays "to study English." He says that
he found it odd that the writer always seemed to be doing housework, his
wife always writing.

†Not to be confused with Elsa's married name-to-be, Mrs. Edward
Seaman.

Lawrence to bar Frieda from his bed—and he did so for one night.

Frieda refused to forgive Ada for this insult and smoldered at Lawrence for weeks. Emile Delavenay, the Lawrence scholar, believes that these angry scenes between the sisters-in-law have never been fully elucidated. Lawrence and Ada, says Delavenay, knew by then that Frieda was Ravagli's mistress, and Ada was also convinced that Lawrence was not being decently nursed and fed. Frieda felt that Lawrence's sisters hated her as the woman who had lured Lawrence away from the bosom of the family. Delavenay interviewed Frieda in 1932 about this episode (and others) and concludes that the quarrel, "if not openly about her sex life, was about her suitability as housewife and nurse" to a sick man.*

Whatever the cause may have been, the quarreling and the commotion depressed Lawrence, already suffering from a "bout with the flu," and he writes to a friend:

> I feel absolutely swamped, must go away by myself for a bit, or I shall give up the ghost. . . . Somehow everything feels in a great muddle, with daughters that are by no means mine, and a sister who doesn't see eye to eye with F. What a trial families are!

Frieda's good nature was not improved when Lawrence's old typewriter arrived from Capri, posted to him as a favor by

---

*However, Delavenay is not alone in accusing Frieda of unnecessary neglect. An eyewitness, Aldous Huxley, says that Lawrence's life might have been extended had Frieda been more helpful. He writes: "We have given up trying to persuade him [Lawrence] to be reasonable. He doesn't want to be and nobody can persuade him to be—except possibly Frieda. But Frieda is worse than he is. We've told her that she's a fool and a criminal, but it has no more effect than telling an elephant." Robert Nichols the playwright says that Huxley told him that Lawrence said during his last hours, "Frieda, you have killed me."

Brett, whom Frieda had sworn never to see again and whose very name had become hateful to her. Caught in a cross fire of old hostilities, Lawrence decided to seek refuge among his friends on Capri. Quitting a furious Frieda and her daughters, Lawrence accompanied Ada and Mrs. Booth to Monte Carlo, where they wound up the final days of their vacation. He then escorted them over to the northbound train at Nice, and on his way back to Italy, instead of stopping at Spotorno, he continued down the coast to Naples. Crossing the water to Capri, Lawrence was met at the landing stage by Harwood Brewster, the Brewsters' son, and Dorothy Brett. Here is her account of that occasion:

> How pleased you are to see us. A new brown
> overcoat, a new grey suit, a brown Homburg,
> hat, brown shoes—heavens! no wonder I did
> not recognize you. But once again how frail,
> how delicate and collapsed you look. We hail a
> carriage, your suitcases are piled on the small
> seat, and we three squeeze into the back seat,
> facing the driver.

Brett would have enjoyed Lawrence's presence at the Hotel Internazionale, where she was staying, but knowing how he hated hotels, she asked the Brewsters to put him up at their Villa Quattro Venti. During tea in honor of his arrival, Lawrence told his hosts how the electric launch refused to start:

> It turned in circles on its rope. I was sitting in it.
> It whirled around and round like a top and no
> one knew what to do. The sailors shouted and
> gesticulated. Then, for no reason at all, as far as
> I could see, it stopped; then restarted with such
> a jerk that I nearly fell into the sea. They had
> forgotten to unfasten the ropes!

Until the island residents got wind that a lion of English letters was among them, Lawrence could rest or paint quietly in the Brewsters' studio up in the tower of the Quattro Venti. But before long, newspaper reporters were interviewing and photographing him. His presence on Capri thus advertised, Lawrence was drawn into the easy routines and relationships of island life.

One evening he drank wine and sang old English ballads (his favorite was "Mary and Joseph") with Brett and the Brewsters, and on another he gave amusing descriptions of the horses, of Susan his cow, and of ranch life back in New Mexico. Once when there were guests present, he led them in charades and on yet another evening he recounted the story of "The Rocking-Horse Winner," then urged the company to contribute additional stories to a volume that would be called, after the Quattro Venti, *Tales of the Four Winds*. With the proceeds from the book, they could buy a yacht and tour the Mediterranean coast.

At supper, Brett, the Brewsters, and Lawrence would talk about their various childhoods. Lawrence gave a "vivid and very terrible picture" of his early life. "At times," said Lawrence, "my mother hardly knew what to do, how to manage. You do not know, Brett, you have never experienced certain things owing to your upbringing; you never can know. My eldest brother died, I believe, because of those early days of semi-starvation, of never having enough clothes, enough warmth, enough to eat. He died of pneumonia, while overworking, and he was, I always think, even more brilliant than I am."

During the day, he went walking with Brett and calling on friends. Among those whom he visited were Mary Cannan, the Francis Brett Youngs, John Ellington Brooks, the Branfords, whose little daughter Dot mistook the bearded guest for "Father Christmas," and Faith Mackenzie at the Casa Solitaria—which Lawrence said was not the same with her husband off on his Channel Island of Herm. While they hiked over the narrow paths of Capri, Lawrence confided to Brett how much his illness had drained him, how he had "crawled away with Ada" as soon as he had recovered, and how "tired to death" he was of the constant feuding with Frieda. "You have no idea, Brett, how humiliating it is to beat a woman," he said.

At the Marina Piccola and other sandy coves, he would stop to rest, possibly as exhausted by having to shout into Brett's ear trumpet as by descending the uneven stone steps to the sea, and say things like, "My life is unbearable. I feel I cannot stand it any longer."

On one occasion, he and Brett clambered up to the Rock of Tiberius, from whence the Roman emperor had thrown his enemies into the sea, and as they ate their picnic lunch at the Tiberio Inn, they talked of "the feeling of unreality, of the old days of glory," that Italy gave them. "Think," said Lawrence, "of Pan, of the mythical Gods; think of all that old mythology; of Lorenzo the Magnificent. That is what Italy and Greece mean to me."

A little later, Lawrence dozed off. The pagan spirit of the place must have affected Brett. She wrote:

> As I watch you, the meaningless modern suit seems to drop away. A leopard skin, a mass of flowers and leaves wrap themselves around you. Out of your thick hair, two small horns poke their sharp points; the slender, cloven hoofs lie entangled in weeds. The flute slips from your hand. I stare at you in a kind of trance.

Later, at her hotel, Brett showed Lawrence her painting of the Crucifixion. In the background is the deep blue Mediterranean, in the foreground, the top of the tower of Quattro

Venti. By the foot of the cross, tempting Christ with a bunch of grapes, Pan reclines. Both Christ's head and Pan's resemble Lawrence's. Brett would be portrayed in a less complimentary light as Dolly in "The Princess." And even his host and hostess would receive a curious kind of undeserved comeuppance in "Things," a story of two Americans in Italy who are inordinately attached to their possessions.

After three weeks under the sun of Capri, Lawrence regained his strength, and by mid-March, felt sufficiently energetic to contemplate a tour of the Etruscan cities accompanied by Millicent Beveridge, who had done his portrait in Taormina, and her friend Mabel Harrison. He may have had in mind some sort of illustrated book, similar to *Sea and Sardinia*. With Brett in tow, he crossed over to Amalfi, where they were met by the two women, and all four of them went up the long, steep twisting climb to Ravello together. At the Hotel Palumbo (once the bishop's palace and now the residence of the Duca di Angro), Lawrence consumed a large steak as an antidote to the Brewsters' vegetarian regime, and then saw to it that he and Brett were assigned separate but adjacent quarters.*

Brett has recorded the events of that first evening:

> Lawrence suddenly walked into my room in his dressing gown. "I do not believe in a relationship unless there is a physical relationship as well," he said. I was frightened as well as excited. He got into my bed, turned and kissed me. I can still feel the softness of his beard, still feel the tension, still feel the overwhelming de-

---

*The proprietor of the hotel, Rufolo, recalls Lawrence as a "small dirty man who coughed a lot" and his companion as a "large blond woman," no doubt confusing Brett with Frieda, whom he would see with Lawrence the following year. He also told me that Lawrence would sit for long periods by himself "on a small rock in front of San Francisco chapel, meditating with a book in his hands." (Letter in my possession)

> sire to be adequate. I was passionately eager to
> be successful, but I had no idea what to do.
> Nothing happened. Suddenly Lawrence got up.
> "It's no good," he said, and stalked out of the
> room. I was devastated, helpless, bewildered.

Lawrence tried again the next night with no better results, and they decided that it would be best if they parted. However, Lawrence seems to have spent a portion of his ten days at Ravello in Brett's company. They went hiking together and once wandered over to the Villa Cimbrone. There in the garden they came across a statue of a blue Venus and each of them rendered it on canvas. "My eye catches the sight of a white violet," Brett recalls. "I pick it and hand it to you [Lawrence]. You hold it with that strange tenderness that flowers bring to your hands."

But Lawrence was growing tired of tenderness with Brett—"Conversations were not easy as I was so deaf in those days," Brett told me in a letter. She was supposed to pick up her visa to the United States, which was waiting for her in Naples. Could she delay her departure for a few days? No, said Lawrence, and sternly ordered her to leave on schedule. As her steamer slipped out of Amalfi harbor, Lawrence waved farewell to her with a blue-and-green scarf she had given him as a keepsake. It was the last time he was to see her, although he continued to correspond with her and even to confide in her.

A week after Brett's departure, Lawrence and his two women friends started north, traveling leisurely through Rome, Perugia, Assisi, Florence, Ravenna, and Venice. Perugia made him want to return for a longer visit and the mosaics of Ravenna impressed him enormously (so says Peter Quennell, who ran into him there), but Assisi, despite the beautiful lower church of St. Francis and the two Giottos, was disappointing after Perugia ("I wouldn't care to live in

Assisi—it's too museumish"). The rather sour memory of
Venice would be revived while he was writing the third
version of *Lady Chatterley*, one or two poems about bathing,
and the story called "None of That," with its Venetian
setting.

After more than six weeks of travel Lawrence was ready
to rest. He had sent Frieda a drawing of Jonah and the whale,
with the caption, "Who is going to swallow whom?" Frieda
was still angry with Lawrence, but her daughters were so
delighted by his long-distance humor and good spirits that
they persuaded their mother to terminate the feud. On April
2, 1926, dressed up in their festive best, the three women
met him at the train and for the remainder of the weekend,
treated him like "the Easter lamb." The day after his return,
he wrote to his mother-in-law that he was going to Perugia
and Florence again: "for six to eight weeks. I think I would
like to write a book about Umbria and the Etruscans, half
travel-book, also scientific."

During the next week or so, a strange confusion occurred.
In Naples, Brett must have learned of Lawrence's plan to
make Perugia his temporary address (letters to several
friends contain this information). Instead of returning to
Capri, she notified him by telegram that she was moving to
Perugia. Blandly Lawrence advised her to "look at Etruscan
things" at the university museum and made it clear that he
did not intend to come down to Perugia while she was there.
In less than a week, Brett was back in Capri ("How quickly
you've moved!" Lawrence remarks innocently from the
safety of Spotorno). Now free to let himself "hanker after
Umbria," Lawrence urged Richard Aldington to come and do
a bit of "Etruscan deciphering" with him on the circuit of
Cortona, Viterbo, Volumni, and Orvieto. This letter ends
with a satiric thrust at "dear heroic Mussolini," with his "Su,
cari miei, su! viveti pericolosamente!" (roughly, "Onward,
my dears, onward! Live dangerously!") Neither of them

made this trip, but Lawrence was leaning toward a summer in the Umbrian region.

On April 19, 1926, the Lawrences and the Weekley girls packed their belongings and bade Angelo Ravagli and Giovanni "*Arrivederci!*" The foursome came down to Florence, where they had reserved rooms at the Pensione Lucchesi on the Lungarno della Zecca (now a first-class hotel), across the river from Nelly Morrison's apartment. They looked up their old friends and Lawrence made a date to have dinner with Reggie Turner. Turner forgot to come and Lawrence sat in Gambrinus's café until eight o'clock, then gave up. Instead of an ugly note, he sent Turner "regrets for the lost evening." The following day he wrote:

> I certainly *heard* Thursday, because I went straight down your stairs and told my wife and the girls, Thursday evening with Reggie. But I have to confess, it once happened to me in Mexico City, with the one man I really liked in that damnable town."*

However, Lawrence didn't care much for Florence this time—the weather was "perfectly vile" and the dripping city seemed not only overcrowded with tourists but also "out of sorts with the present regime." He wasn't sure he wanted to be anywhere in Italy under Fascism—it wasn't nearly "so jolly as it used to be," and he wondered about heading for Tunis, Dalmatia, Ragusa, the Balearic Islands, Castelvetrano in Sicily, and even to Soviet Russia (he had been studying Russian so that he could work with Koteliansky on Bunin, Shestov, and Dostoevski). Frieda was feeling equally restless

---

*Lawrence is referring to a missed meeting with Somerset Maugham. On that occasion, Maugham "said Thursday, and I heard Friday (I still believe he said Friday)" (letter, May 1, 1926).

and couldn't decide whether she wanted to visit her parents when her daughters left for London or remain in Italy (the girls left on April 28). Pino Orioli, the bookseller, resolved the issue for them: he had been 'keeping an eye open for suitable quarters in the area and recommended a *villino* about seven miles west of Florence. The place was not easy to find. After taking the number 16 tram from the Duomo to the end of the line at Vingone, they walked almost a mile to a lane flanked by two cypresses, turned off there into a sort of valley, and then eventually came up again to face "a big square box of a house on the crown of the hill near the church of San Paolo Mosciano." For Frieda it was love at first sight:

> On top of one of those Tuscan hills stood a villa. My heart went out to it . . . so perfectly placed, with a panorama of the Valdarno in front, Florence on the left, and the umbrella-pine woods behind.

Lawrence made inquiries of the *padrone*, a *capitano di Cavalleria* named Raul Mirenda, who came out to Scandicci with his wife only once a week. He agreed to let Lawrence the second floor of the villa, with an option to renew the lease, for 3000 lire a year (about a hundred dollars). Probably about May 8 the Lawrences moved into the Villa Mirenda, their home (except for occasional absences) for the next three years.

Almost immediately Lawrence invited Reggie Turner to lunch and asked him to bring Pino Orioli with him. On the possibility that Turner might come alone, he furnished detailed directions for getting to the villa and provided a rough map as well.

Within a short time, Lawrence had established good relationships with the three peasant families on the Mirenda estate: the Orsinis, the Bandellis, and the Pinis. The Pinis'

eldest daughter, sixteen-year-old Giulia, came to work for
the Lawrences as a domestic, and both of them grew to love
her cheerful spirits and her peasant wisdom—after leaving
Italy, Lawrence wrote to her regularly.

Unusually heavy rains during the first two weeks made
the Lawrences long for the "dry sun" of Sicily or New Mexico and confined their activities to fixing up their quarters,
which had "about five sticks of furniture in its big old brick-
floored rooms." With Giulia and her brother Pietro acting as
guides, they shopped around in Florence for the things they
required to make the house more habitable. Before long,
Lawrence had built a kitchen table and put up brackets for
pots and pans. Together they painted the shutters and the
chairs, laid grass mats on the floor, and sprayed the walls
with white calcimine (later, they would be decorated with
Lawrence's paintings, one of them having Pietro as a model),
and generally made the "old place look more alive."

In *Adventures of a Bookseller*, Orioli writes this about the place
he recommended to his friends: ". . . a distant and dilapidated
place among the hills with no water supply and only one
small fireplace. Well I knew the Villa Mirenda in summer
and winter, well I remember that endless tram-ride and then
the walk up!" Orioli says that Lawrence "managed his own
washing and scrubbing and mending and needle-work and
cooking and marketing" very successfully, disappointing the
peasant family that hoped to make money off him. Orioli is
often unkind in this book, concluding that Lawrence was a
homosexual gone wrong. Aldington warns that parts of this
memoir may have been written or rewritten by a spiteful
Norman Douglas.

Nearby in another *villino* there lived an English family
named Wilkinson, whom Lawrence found amusing, especially Gair, the paterfamilias, who had "the wildest red
beard, sticking out all around." Under the direction of Gair's
brother Walter, the family used to give puppet shows in the

villages in England, performing plays they had written themselves. "Rather fun!" Lawrence exclaimed when he learned about it. "I want them to bring a caravan and puppets here, and I'll go with them and bang the drum, in the Italian villages." Of course, nothing came of Lawrence's fantasy, but the two families remained on good terms until the Wilkinsons moved into Florence in November because Mrs. Wilkinson got tired of cooking. Lawrence tried unsuccessfully to persuade the Brewsters to take the *villino*.

As summer approached and the rains relented, Lawrence and Frieda, basking on their balcony in the hot sunshine, watched Tuscany flower and unfold its natural mysteries. Below them in the gardens of the villa, "the lovely slopes of vines and olives [seemed to] glow green in the pure air." The fruit was beginning to ripen: big apricots called *fiori*, peaches, plums, little pears, and grapes still green and hard. The riot of anemones, tulips, and lavender reminded Frieda of the ground in a Fra Angelico painting. In the distance, they could see threshers at work, and the sheaves of wheat drying in the sun made them think of "people dead asleep in the heat." The bells of the little church of San Paolo behind them would ring midday, and after lunch, in the peasant custom, the Lawrences would take an afternoon siesta.

Sometimes they would tramp through the unspoiled, colorful countryside, Lawrence in shirt, trousers, and sandals, Frieda in a cotton dress. There were carpets of violets in the woods and clusters of primroses in the valleys. They could hear the girls singing in the fields as they cut grain, while the cicadas, "like little sewing machines in the leafy trees," shrilled in counterpoint. Returning home with the oxen at sundown, they would listen to the ballads that the peasants beat out as they drew water for the chores. In the cool of the evening, the nightingales would start singing again while Lawrence rested, read, or wrote letters. After two months at the Villa Mirenda, Lawrence wrote to Brett:

"Italy is always lovely, and . . . I am sure it is right for me to stay this year in the softness of the Mediterranean."

Did these pleasures of nature begin to pall by that summer? Though isolated in the idyllic, the Lawrences began to seek out the company of their friends in Florence. At least twice a week they would take the little green tram into the city and go shopping. They searched in vain for the rope-soled shoes for Frieda that they had liked so much in Capri—the stores didn't carry her size. When their errands were over, they would spend the remainder of the day calling on the old faithful of the English colony and making new friends, such as the Franchettis and the Fasolas. When the couple would return to the country, arms laden with parcels, one of the young *contadini* with the pony trap would meet them at Vingone and take them up the road to their home.

Lawrence visited Reggie Turner and probably Norman Douglas several times and lunched with "the world's champion fencer" ("How's that?" he boasted to Koteliansky). One afternoon he and Frieda visited Edith Sitwell's parents, "a queer couple" who lived in a castle fifteen miles away at Montegufoni. The senior Sitwell must have regarded Frieda as equally queer. After luncheon, before his horrified gaze, she jumped on all the superb seventeenth-century beds to see if the mattresses were soft, and when she signed her name in the visitors' book, she put after her signature, "Geborene" and then something that Sitwell senior could not read. "So extraordinary!" he told his daughter when she came to the castle for a visit. "Of *course* she was born. Everybody is." He also described Lawrence as "most extraordinary," but Lawrence did not find him or the other expatriates very exciting (". . . all the better. I don't ask excitement"). Though "overrun with tourists" and "irritable to a degree with fascism," Florence remained for Lawrence "one of the most intimate towns in the world," and he gave up its pleasures only because of his ill health.

During the summer of 1926, he and Frieda played host to a number of diverse visitors, among them Reggie Turner, Pino Orioli, possibly the Huxleys, and Gerald Hugh Tyrwhitt-Wilson, the 14th Baron Berners, a novelist, musician and painter who invited the Lawrences to stay with him in Rome during October and to be motored around to the Etruscan places. Lawrence thought that he was "too rich: Rolls Roycey" and decided to decline the invitation (he was already bothered by the "unholy bunch of rich Americans" in the area). Angelo Ravagli wanted to pay a visit, but confined to his new station at Porto Maurizio, near Trieste,* he could only write dolorous letters.

Requests for another novel came from both Secker and Knopf—despite a poor press, *The Plumed Serpent* was enjoying a brisk sale—but Lawrence was losing his enthusiasm and energy for hard work, even for the Etruscan project that he had so long nursed in his heart. "Why should I write books for any of 'em! I had enough . . . they can whistle." He decided to live close to the chest, independent of publishers' requests, and to limit his activity on the typewriter (newly reconditioned) to preparing Frieda's German translation of his play, *David.*†

---

*Frieda's mysterious visits to Trieste were trysts with Ravagli.

†General Mirenda told me that during this period Lawrence was frequently sick (which may account for his modestly productive stay at Scandicci). Nevertheless, the general found him to be a "beautiful man in the spirit" and became very fond of the "eccentric" English writer. Lawrence had learned Italian and often the two would converse about the world and the state of Italy. The couple often took their meals with the Mirendas, and the general said that he once had many letters and other Lawrence memorabilia that were lost or destroyed during the war. Carlo Levi's contention that Lawrence was regarded by Italians as "one of the large number of bizarre Englishmen who had pitched their tents in this eternal landscape" seems unjust.

In mid-July they left Florence for Germany and England. They reached Baden-Baden for the baroness's seventy-fifth birthday, spent two weeks there, and went over to London. There Lawrence renewed his acquaintance with Aldous Huxley, whom he had met in 1915—they were to become fast friends. In August, after they had visited his family on the Lincolnshire coast and had spent some time in Scotland and Skye, he and Frieda returned to London for two weeks. Following a stopover in Paris, they came down directly to Florence on October 4, just in time for the final stages of the *vendemmia* (the grape harvest). Despite the sourish smell that arose from the grapes already gathered in the cellar, Lawrence was glad to "sit in the big empty room and be peaceful" once again.

Chapter 8

FOR most of that Tuscan fall, Lawrence lived quietly, watching with a "warm, friendly familiarity the farm workers in their daily occupation," writing a little by whim, but perfectly content to drift with the soft, sunny days turning pleasantly cool. While Frieda would be making jam and jelly, he would putter around the villa or sit in the garden observing the birds that came to call before heading south and the butterflies that would "sit content on my shoe." He was enchanted by the numerous nightingales in "the little leafy woods." Sometimes, while he and Frieda were having an altercation, "the chief nightingale would swell and go at it like Caruso in the Third Act—simply a brilliant burbling frenzy of music, singing you down, till you simply can't hear yourself speak or quarrel" ("The Nightingale," *Forum*, September 1927). At other times, he would walk by himself in the woods, perhaps pondering his next painting or poem as he strode past the pink cyclamen and the wild strawberries in bloom. Political tensions were growing in northern Italy, but the rhythms of his life were simple, tranquil, and undisturbed by the outside world except for sometimes unwelcome news in the mail and welcome visits from friends.

Early in October, Richard Aldington and Dorothy Yorke*

---

*A young woman from Reading, Pennsylvania, with artistic aspirations, Dorothy Yorke first met the Lawrences in London during World War I, came to stay for a few days (". . . hope they won't mind the hard beds," Lawrence writes before their arrival). Though Dorothy Yorke remembers him as gaunt and tired in appearance, to Aldington he appeared at his "freshest and most charming." If either harbored resentment over the faintly derisive portraits of them in *Aaron's Rod* as Josephine and Robert Cunningham, it must have been dissolved by his cheerful courage and relaxed hospitality. One golden afternoon, while the women were in Florence, the two men sat out under the chestnut trees and talked about "this and that," more interested in the peasant children than in the conversation. Every now and then a shy little barefooted child would slip through the shrubbery with a bunch of grapes in his fists. "Pretend not to see," Lawrence would whisper as the child crept stealthily toward them over the grass, like a little animal. Then Lawrence would look up, feigning surprise, would ask, *"Che vuoi?"* ("What do you want?") The child would answer, *"Niente* ("Nothing"), *Signore Lorenzo." "Vieni qui"* ("Come here"), Lawrence would command, and when the boy presented the grapes, he would then say, *"Ma, cosa hai li?"* ("But what have you there?") *"Uva* ("Grapes"), *Signore Lorenzo,"* the child would respond. *"Per me?"* ("For me?") *"Si signore."* Then Lawrence, no matter how tired, would go into the house to get the child a piece of chocolate. He would apologize to Aldington for the apparent overgenerosity (at *vendemmia* grapes are without value and chocolate is always a luxury) by explaining how poor the peasants were and how much their children needed sugar for their health. On another occasion, while Walter Wilkinson was visiting him, he cured a child's toothache by offering the howling infant a bag of sweets which he always seemed to carry on him.

_____

while they were living in the Aldingtons' quarters at 44 Mecklenburgh Square. She occupied the attic of that building. She was to be among the founders of Rananim.

Often they visited and were visited by Pino Orioli and Reggie Turner ("Really, he's getting quite gaga!"). Right after Aldington and Dorothy Yorke left Florence (he was to see them several more times before their departure), Aldous and Maria Huxley called at the Villa Mirenda. Lawrence had read with admiration some essays Huxley had written on Italian travel and had suggested that they meet again. Since the Huxleys were in Florence in late October, they drove over in their new car, with Maria carrying four old canvases as a gift to their host. They spent a pleasant day together (a couple of walks, a picnic with Vernon Lee, the writer on Italian art and Italy, a meal at a nearby *trattoria*), and before leaving, Huxley offered to let Lawrence buy his old car. Lawrence replied that he had "no desire to scud about the face of the country . . . struggling with a machine." It was much preferable, he thought, to live "heroically *a la* Frieda," painting miles of window frames and acres of doors, or to go quietly into the pinewoods and write.

The Florence visit was the cementing point of a friendship between Lawrence and the Huxleys. Between Lawrence and Maria there was a straight intuitive affinity; they got on right away. Maria loved him and Lawrence, in Huxley's words, was "very fond of her." They had much fun together, though Frieda could irritate Huxley. Despite his suspicion that Huxley's *One or Two Graces* "or whatever it is," contained "an unflattering character of me," Lawrence was touched by the kindness and sympathy of the young writer, and from that time until his death, they were often together—again in Scandicci in March, in Florence, in Forte dei Marmi, in Bandol, and finally in Vence.

In early November, Angelo Ravagli, now a captain, came for a day from Gradisca in the Udine district "and descended on [Lawrence] with a dense fog of that peculiar inert Italian misery," causing him to comment that "the Italians are certainly more dreary than the English, just now." To recover from the impact of Ravagli's visit, Lawrence painted "a nice big picture" of women that his vegetarian friends, the Wilkinsons, were afraid to look at because it was "too 'suggestive.'" In a letter to Martin Secker, he asks plaintively, "Why do vegetarians always behave as if the world was vegetably propagated, even?"

About this time, perhaps encouraged by Huxley, Lawrence began to write a long short story (so says Frieda) about the conflict between the soul and animal in man, no doubt the first version of *Lady Chatterley's Lover*. Here is Frieda's account of its origins:

> After breakfast . . . he would take his book and pen and a cushion, followed by John the dog, and go into the woods behind Mirenda and come back to lunch with what he had written. I read it day by day and wondered how his chapters were built up and how it all came to him.

Sitting once more on a rock warmed by the sun, he would be distracted by a shepherd calling his sheep with weird, grunting noises on a tin flute, and then would whistle a vague little tune of his own in order to focus his thoughts more effectively. This afternoon pastime may have been made perilous by the hunters banging away at the little birds going south "like the fools and countrymen of St. Francis they are." The sight of an Italian "going to the death of something or someone" may have wakened in Lawrence some apprehension about the Fascist mood which was spreading across Italy "like some plague." On the other hand, the *virilisso uccelino*, in his "velvet corduroys, bandolier, cartridges, and game-bag over his shoulder" ("Man Is a Hunter," *Atlantic Monthly*, February 1927, reprinted in *Phoenix*) may have provided him with a rough model for one of his characters, the swarthy, gun-carrying gamekeeper called Parkin (later Oliver Mellors).

By the end of November, the hot spell ended and Lawrence could no longer work comfortably in the woods. He wrote instead on his balcony, from where he could see the "wide yellow floods in the Arno valley" and the snow-capped Apennines to the west, the same mountains he had seen from the other side in 1913. When the air became too nippy, he retired into the sitting room, which a good woodburning stove had turned into a "quite nice and comfortable refuge" against the cold. Seated on one of the Vallambrosa chairs at the table he had built himself, he continued to work away at his novel. According to Raul Mirenda, he used to interpose tasks of a domestic nature among his intellectual occupations: he would repair the collars of his own shirts, iron them, weave straw hats, and sometimes cook dinner. Once, while he was preoccupied with his writing, one of the local dogs sneaked into the house, seized a lamb roast he was preparing, and out of Lawrence's reach, munched on it. "Today Geppurillo [the dog] will eat better than we," Lawrence observed philosophically.

Christmas, however, was a satisfying interlude with the peasants. Assisted by Pietro and Giulia Pini, the Lawrences trimmed a tree (cut fresh that morning by Pietro*) with tinsel, candles, gold and silver cones, and then hung it with wooden toys for the peasant children, many of whom had never seen such trinkets before. Twenty-seven of the country folk were invited to the celebration of the holiday, English-style, and in the evening, while the children played with their toys, the fathers smoked long Otscanos and the women drank sweet wine.

---

*Pietro Pini may have served as the model for the painting called *Contadini*, which Lawrence was to finish in Gsteig in 1928.

Writing the new novel, breaking with old conventions, must have put a strain on Lawrence (he complains about an "inner *vivi pericolosamente*"). For diversion, he turned his attention to another activity: "If Maria Huxley had not come rolling up to our house with four rather large canvasses, one which she had busted . . . I might never have started in on a real picture in my life. But those nice stretched canvasses were too tempting. We had been painting doors and window-frames in the house, so there was a little stock of oils, turps, and colour in powder, such as one buys from an Italian *drogheria*." He mixed his paints in little casseroles, and used not only the brushes left over from the last house-painting, but also his fingers and the palms of his hands to apply his fleshly tints and brilliant colors. He did a "nice biggish picture" of a man and a woman in a pink room with a child looking up, called *The Unholy Family* (he described it as "*molto moderno!*"), another "long one, about 1½ yards by ¾ yard, of Boccaccio's story of the gardener and the nunnery," still another called *The Fight with the Amazons*, and by Christmas he was painting the last of that series. While hanging them on the wall of the sitting room, he concluded that "painting is more fun and less soul work than writing."

In mid-January of 1927, the Lawrences received a package from Mabel Dodge Luhan containing herbs that smelled of Taos. When they went into the *trattoria* in Vingone, the *padrona* kept sniffing: "*Ces e? ma cos a questo profumo?*" ("What is that odor?") until Lawrence opened the parcel and gave her a bit. The parcel reminded him that he had promised Mrs. Luhan that he would send her some books from the library at the Curonia, her old Florentine villa behind the Piazza Michelangelo. He and Orioli went over one day and discovered that Harold Acton had told Pietro the caretaker that Mrs. Luhan was dead. Lawrence assured Pietro that Acton had greatly exaggerated and the joyful Pietro sent her "*rangraziamente e ricordi*," ("Many thanks and regards."). Lawrence had heard that Edwin Dodge wished to sell the villa for a hundred thousand dollars but guessed that he would be lucky to get half that figure, even though it was a "lovely place" that he would not have been loathe to occupy himself.

About a week later, Earl Brewster arrived from Capri for a visit of two days. He recounted his experience in India to Lawrence (who had now become interested in Hinduism) and then took him to see Albert Magnelli, the abstractionist painter who was exhibiting in Florence. To Lawrence, Magnelli seemed "very self-important and arch-priestly, worse than Gertler." Though his paintings had been highly praised by critics, Lawrence had severe reservations about them too:

> The modern artists, who make art out of antipathy to life, always leave me feeling a little sick. It is as if they used all their skill and their efforts to dress up a skeleton. Magnelli has lovely colour and design—but underneath it is empty, he pins all his beauty on to a dead nothingness. What's the good. I think I learned something from him—but rather what not to be, than what to be.

What he learned he sought to express in his next group of paintings, *Men Bathing*, *Red Willow Trees*, *Eve Regaining Paradise*, and *Resurrection*. With all their technical imperfections, they catch that quality Lawrence believed all healthy art should reflect, "the whole sensual self."

Sensing that Lawrence was a brilliantly gifted amateur, Brewster, during their walks together in the Tuscan hills, encouraged him to continue with his painting. Lawrence in turn urged Brewster, who had given up his house on Capri, to take a villa in the vicinity, but since nothing suitable was vacant, Brewster returned to Capri. No sooner had he left than Lawrence also felt an inclination to go south, as though Brewster "had been putting his will over" on him. He had finished the last part of *Lady Chatterley I,* his most comprehensive attempt to portray in writing "the whole sensual self" of a man and woman relationship. On March 18, sufficiently recuperated from another attack of flu, he started out for Ravello, where the Brewsters had rented the Palazzo Cimbrone from Lord Grimthorpe (Frieda had already left for Germany). En route, he stayed for two days in Rome with Christine Hughes and her daughter, Mary Christine, Americans whom he had known in New Mexico. The daughter persuaded the mother to drive them over to Ostia to see the Castle of the Caesars and the ancient fortifications. Lawrence describes the journey in "Laura Philippine" (*Phoenix II*), one of his most delightful yet penetrating pieces of light prose, using Mary as the model for the jazz-addicted, cigarette-smoking, languid Laura.

Lawrence had visited Palazzo Cimbrone once before, with Brett. This time he enjoyed the spectacular setting for a full week. The spacious villa is surrounded by formal gardens of shrubbery and flower beds, with fountains and statuary spaced throughout. A path from the palazzo leads through the gardens to a lookout, from where one can see the red-tile rooftops of Sorrento below and in the distance the hump of Capri.

During the cool but sunny days, Lawrence would stroll with Brewster through these gardens, once revisiting the Blue Venus, another time encountering a modern Eve which displeased him so much that he covered it with mud. He told Brewster that the new statues of Niobe and Mercury were "promiscuous." What Lawrence may have meant was that their sexuality lacked the mystery and beauty of the great phallic iconography which represented for him the "deep, deep life which has been denied in us." He and Brewster made plans for the long-discussed pilgrimage to the Etruscan cities. Among the remains of those fascinating people whom the Romans had destroyed, Lawrence hoped to discover some sign, some revelation of those lost phallic mysteries "denied in us." He broadened his reading of the acknowledged authorities on the subject, including P. Ducati's *Etruria Antica* (which he found worthless); D. Randall-MacIver's *Villanovans and Early Etruscans*; George Dennis's *Cities and Cemeteries of Etruria* (all three he found "rather boring, repetitions and conjectures"), and Fritz Weege's *Etruskische Malerie*, which he wanted for its reproductions.

In the evenings, when he was not reading, Lawrence lounged before a log fire with his friends, told tales about his early days in Eastwood, played games like charades and hide-and-seek with Brewster's boy, and sang Wagnerian opera. As his health improved, his interest in painting revived. He had planned to do a canvas of the Crucifixion, with Pan and some nymphs as part of the background, but perhaps because Etruscan phallic consciousness dominated his thoughts, he omitted the Crucifixion and retained the pagan deities disporting themselves in a distinctly un-Christlike manner. He told Earl Brewster that he was putting a phallus somewhere in each one of his other paintings.

When the weather grew milder in early April, he and Brewster drove out to the end of the Sorrentine peninsula, walked back to the town of Sorrento, and then set out on the journey which Lawrence would describe in *Etruscan Places*, his third book of Italian travel. As they made their way along the Amalfitan coast, Lawrence would gaze longingly out to the sea and speak about recovering "a lost self, Mediterranean, anterior to us," and en route to the Maremma Romana, where the Etruscans had built their cities of wood, Lawrence told Brewster about the new novel brewing in his imagination, based upon an almost forgotten incident in Cornwall, including an aristocratic lady and her cowman. In Rome, they stopped at the papal museum to inspect the Etruscan remains. Infused with the archaeological spirit, they arrived by train at Palo, "a station in nowhere," walked five miles to Cerveteri, and lunched in a "deep cavern where mule drivers were drinking brackish wine." As Lawrence and Brewster were consuming their broth and tripe, there swaggered into the cavern a "spurred shepherd wearing goat-skin trousers." His face was faunlike, a "brown, rather still straight-nosed face with a little black moustache and often a little tuft of black beard, yellow eyes, rather shy under long lashes, but able to glare with quiet glare, on occasion, and mobile lips that had a queer way of showing the teeth when talking, bright white teeth." It occurred to Lawrence that one rarely saw that sort of face in Italy anymore because all the faun faces had been killed in the war. The unexpected guest may have reminded him of some of the Italians he had described in *Twilight in Italy* and of his own faun-faced creation in *The Rainbow*, Anthony, the brother of Winifred.

In Cerveteri, they saw their first Etruscan tombs. Led by a guide carrying an acetylene lamp, they descended into these vaults of living rock and explored the chambers where the aristocrats of the city had been laid to rest, with the interred ashes of their attendants to keep them company. These tombs had been designed with a simplicity that had "the natural beauty of the phallic consciousness." The red-painted male figures on the walls ("For they are dancing") inspired "The Argonauts" and the little bronze bark that bore the dead to the other world suggested the central image of his greatest poem, "The Ship of Death."

Lawrence learned what death meant to the Etruscans: it was neither confinement to the fires of hell nor ascent to heavenly paradise, but a continuation of physical existence, a perpetuation of the life of phallic consciousness symbolized, at the doors of the tombs, by columns, by "phallic stones" beautifully carved, and by lingams cut out of the rock and fitted into sockets. For the Etruscans, death apparently meant a life of perpetual fornication (it is small wonder that the Etruscans depicted on tombs are always smiling).

That evening, they caught the train to Civitavecchia. The once-genial land, Lawrence observed, had changed:

> The smitten sea has sunk and fallen back, the
> weary land has emerged when, apparently, it
> didn't want to, and the flowers of the coastline
> are miserable bathing-places such as Ladispoli
> and seaside Ostia, desecration put upon desola-
> tion, to the triumphant trump of the mosquito.

At Civitavecchia, they took rooms at a hotel nearby the station, but only after some difficulty with a passport official who made Lawrence furious: "Those poor rats at Ladispoli had seen me and B. go back to the train. And this was enough to rouse their suspicions, I imagine, so they tele-graphed to Civitavecchia. Why are officials always fools? Even when there is no war on? What could they imagine we were doing?"

Early the next morning, the two travelers caught the train, without further mishap, to Tarquinia, once the metrop-olis of Etruria, with "its towers pricking up like antennae on the side of a low bluff of a hill, some few miles inland from the sea." Not far from Gentile's Inn, where they were staying, was the museum of the Palazzo Vitelleschi. As they entered, they were saluted in the Fascist manner, *alla Romana*. "Why," mused Lawrence, "don't they discover the Etruscan salute, and salute us *all' Etrusca?*" After an after-noon of examining the great sarcophagi and burial urns, they explored the painted tombs. The stuccoed walls of these remarkable burial vaults were almost alive with the still vivid paintings of hunters, birds, bulls, lions, and lovers. Two bits of *pornografico* in the Tomb of the Bull arrested his attention, one in particular which showed a ruddy Etruscan apparently engaged in the act of anal intercourse with a young woman. All of this was enormously stimulating for Lawrence, and he was puzzled by the German archaeologist who made the tour with them. Whenever Lawrence proposed some subtle interpretation of the symbolism in the Etruscan paintings, the German protested that they meant "nothing, nothing," and despite his insistence that Vulci offered even less to see, Lawrence and Brewster decided that the opposite must be true. Lawrence wanted to visit the Tomb of Isis, allegedly the burial place of an Etruscan noblewoman. So by train they "rattled up to the little town" of Montalto di Castro, and from there a cart bore them over a rutted road toward the tombs of Vulci. On the way, they saw a bridge and a castle of black *tufo*, the sole remains of where the city once stood. They got out to explore with their driver Luigi, "intelligent as a wild thing," and encountered some "queer-looking men, youngish fellows, smallish, unshaven, dirty; not peasants but workmen of some sort, who looked as if they had been swept together among the rubbish." They were laborers, employed in one of Mussolini's irrigation projects. Lawrence couldn't stand "their feeling of suspicion and almost of opposition," and made no attempt to converse as he habitually did with Italians whom he met while traveling. A new order was taking over.

When the pair reached their destination, they went from tomb to tomb, sometimes forced to wriggle on their bellies, nonetheless awed by the black damp chambers that once housed the dead of the small but rich city of the Etruscan league. Most of their treasure had been transported to the museums of the Vatican, of Fiesole, and London, and what had been left behind in the "damp grisly darkness" was mainly the excavation rubble and broken rubbish. In the Tomb of Isis, what Lawrence missed most of all was the statue of a lady which Dennis, an authority on the Etruscans, thought was surely Egyptian.

On the way back to the railroad station, with the "bright sea-wind blowing over the Maremma and the men travelling away from work on horseback, on mules or on asses," Lawrence forgot for a moment the poverty and ignorance of the people living on this stagnant marshland and said to Luigi, "It would be a good life, to live here, and have a house on the hills, and a horse to ride, and space, except for the malaria."

That night they stayed in Grosseto before proceeding to Volterra, the last city on their Etruscan circuit. On the following morning, Palm Sunday, as they were strolling through the town, Brewster saw in a shop window a toy white rooster escaping from an egg. Jokingly, he suggested the title of "the escaped cock" for a story that Lawrence had conceived about the Resurrection. In the afternoon, they took a "small, forlorn little train" to Saline de Volterra, the famous old saltworks, where they transferred to cog-and-ratchet coach that crept "like a beetle up the slope to the most northerly of the Etruscan cities. Crowning a "towering great bluff of rock that gets all the winds and sees all the world," Volterra seemed to be a "sort of inland island, still curiously isolated, and grim." As they wandered through the "stony stoniness of the medieval town" on that cold gray Sunday of Palms, Lawrence noticed a legend painted on a wall: "*Mussolini ha sempre ragione!*"* ("Mussolini is always right!") Though he believed that Italian politics were none of his business, he commented to himself that the fundamental uneasiness and indecision in the soul of most Italians, their traditional distrust of politicians, would make it more than difficult for anyone to lead them successfully.

Volterra, like Vulci, was disappointing after their earlier experiences. Aside from the city gate, the lone standing reminder of Etruscan glory, only the local museum proved

---

*In "Blessed Are the Powerful," Lawrence is derisive about the Italian dictator: "... a little harmless Glory in baggy trousers—Papa Mussolini ..."

to be interesting. They spent most of the next day gazing at an array of alabaster chests carved with mythological monsters or favorite pastimes to remind the dead of the living. The boar hunt was represented repeatedly on the sides of these indigenous sarcophagi. Since the boar hunt was "still the grandest sport of Italy," these scenes gave Lawrence a sense of historical continuity. Then, a flash of intuition confirmed with great clarity something which he had vaguely suspected: the essential secret of these vanished people, frozen into stone, also survived in the living substance around him (so he tells a friend in a letter). It could be seen, this secret, marvelously in the faces of the peasants he had met at Gargnano, at Fiascherino, on Sardinia, at Scandicci, and now on the road to Vulci—faces "still jovial with Etruscan vitality, beautiful with the mystery of the unrifled ark, ripe with the phallic knowledge and the Etruscan carelessness." One such face decorating a shallow bowl in the Volterra museum inspired Lawrence's drawing that appears as the frontispiece to the Black Sun edition of "Sun"—it shows a ruddy, grinning satanic visage woven into the image of the sun.* Soon such faces would no longer be seen in Italy. Lawrence concludes glumly.

Later that day, the two pilgrims parted, Brewster heading south for Ravello, Lawrence climbing into the bus for Florence. After a dusty, bone-shaking trip that lasted five hours, Lawrence arrived at the Vingone streetcar terminus. There he was greeted by Frieda, who had arrived home a week earlier nursing a cold and a depression. Lawrence was fatigued but exultant. It had been more than a mere journey. Though his interest lay more with physical Italy than with

---

*So he told Caresse Crosby, the copublisher with her husband Harry Crosby of the Black Sun Press. She got to know Lawrence in Paris and had in her possession at her castle in Roccasinebalda, before her death, many mementos of their friendship.

political Italy, Lawrence felt that he had made a significant choice: he threw his lot in with the Italian of Etruscan origin ("altogether without sternness or will power") over the Italian of Roman roots, in whose image Mussolini was seeking to refashion the country. The Romans had never wished to understand the Etruscan spirit: they denied it and obliterated it. Leonardo da Vinci "only bungled the pure Etruscan smile." In brief, the Romans saw "the blood-consciousness" of the Etruscans as evil. The book that emerged from these sketches (published serially in *Travel*, an American magazine, during the winter of 1927–1928) reflects his strong distaste for the Rome worship which was fundamental to the Fascist philosophy. Had he not been writing under Fascism, Lawrence might have written quite differently about the Etruscans. He might have loved them as much, but he would not have had to fight for them so, against the Romans.*

The spring of 1927 came early, and soon Lawrence was back at his favorite haunt in the forest, revising his new novel, *Lady Chatterley*, as the nightingales sang and watched him turn the page of the lined foolscap. Into this third version Lawrence worked his impressions of his latest visit to Venice (Connie goes there for her vacation, instead of Spain, as in the first two versions). And a disguised Michael Arlen was added to the cast of characters.

This rhythm was briefly interrupted in April by the

---

*"For all the men were soldiers or politicians in the Roman spell, assertive, manly, splendid apparently, but of an inward meanness, an inadequacy." (*The Man Who Died* [Vintage]). In *Aaron's Rod*, Sir William Franks says: "I cannot stand, myself, that miserable specimen of the modern Roman. He has most of the vices of the old Romans and none of their virtues." In *Etruscan Places*, we read: "The Romans took the life out of them [the Etruscans]. It seems as if the power of resistance to life, self-assertion and overbearing, such as the Romans knew . . . would always succeed in destroying the natural flowering of life." In spite of its syntax, this passage should settle the question of whether or not Lawrence was sympathetic to Mussolini's pretensions.

appearance of Frieda's daughter. On the fourteenth of the
month, he writes to Baroness von Richthofen, in German:*

> Barbey came Tuesday—and naturally with a
> woman as duenna behind her; otherwise the old
> man [Weekley] would never have let her come.
> We put the woman into a hotel at Vingone, Bar-
> bey stays with us. She is nice, older than last
> year—not so beautiful—tall as a telephone
> pole—and quieter—not much life in her. That is
> London over her . . . It is sad to see her so
> useless, so lifeless.

Barbey's presence (in one letter he says for two weeks, in
another three) caused a "bit of an upset," but Lawrence managed to polish the final version of the novella which still bore
Earl Brewster's title, "The Escaped Cock." In his own words,
it is a "story of the Resurrection, where Jesus gets up and
feels very sick about everything, and can't stand the old
crowd any more—so cuts out—and as he heals up, he begins
to find what an astonishing place the phenomenal world is,
far more marvelous than any salvation or heaven." At the
same time, he was refreshing his memory of the erotic iconography in the tombs by looking at photographs in Fritz
Weege's book and at some other pictures from Alinari, especially the one from the Tomba dei Tori, "the two little
improper bits, *'un poco pornografico'*, as brave as life." What that
last phrase meant the revised *Lady* would reveal soon.

---

*Armin Arnold, "The German Letters of D. H. Lawrence," *Comparative
Literature Studies* (1966), p. 293.

Chapter 9

IN early May, a cable arrived from Mabel Dodge Luhan and Brett inviting the Lawrences and the Brewsters to Taos. Frieda by now could not abide even the thought of Brett, and Lawrence, though he wanted to feel the freedom of the open spaces again, decided that he had better rent the Villa Mirenda for another year. About this time he was afflicted with an attack of malaria. A period of rain piled on his illness and gave him a "spell of loathing for the Italian countryside" and the Italians themselves ("But now they are like cabbages / and people are sad and grim / and all so very mechanical! / oh dear! what's happening to Tuscans!"*). Also the growing hostility toward foreigners that characterized the Fascist regime made him feel a "certain unfreedom," the first serious

---

*From "A La Maniere de D. H. Lawrence," one of the uncollected poems written at about this time. The poem contains the lines, "They have taken off the beautiful red Lily [on the Florence tram] / and put a dirty green large cabage [sic]"—a clue to where Lawrence may have found the name for Rawdon Lilly in his Florentine novel, Aaron's Rod. In "David," an essay probably written in 1926 about the Michelangelo statue on a rainy day, Lawrence says: ". . . Florence the Lily-town . . . Once there was pure equilibrium, and the Lily blossomed. But the Lily now—livid." Furthermore, it is worth noting that "Aaron" is almost an anagram of "Arno" (simply reverse the last two letters and "Aaron" becomes the Italian way of pronouncing "Arno." Thus both Lilly and Aaron are linked to Florence by virtue of their names—a mystical, even magical kind of association that Lawrence no doubt deliberately sought to suggest.

suspicion that "Italy was no place for a *man* to live in." He compared himself to "a fading lily." He tried to complete his painting of the Resurrection, but he admits to Earl Brewster that he had "no guts for anything: *lo spettro di me stesso!*" ("I am a shadow of my former self!").

During these hopeful, heartbreaking months when he was awaiting the health that was never to come, Lawrence corresponded with Mabel Dodge Luhan about her second book, *Intimate Memories*, then in progress. She sent him the manuscript and Lawrence advised her to publish the book in America but to substitute invented names for the real. He told her to distribute it by private subscription, he told her to try having it published in German, he told her to have it printed in Paris with her own funds, he told her to lock the manuscript in a safe-deposit vault for fifty years, he told her to give her papers, sealed, to the French Academy, to be opened after her death, he all but told her to tie them around her neck and go leap into a lake.*

Later that May, Osbert and Edith Sitwell motored over from Montegufoni. Lawrence wrote Richard Aldington in a letter of May 24, 1927, that he liked the Sitwells very much, but Dame Edith, persuaded that Lawrence had poked fun at her family in *Lady Chatterley*, recalls him with malice in *Taken Care Of*:

> Mr. Lawrence looked like a plaster gnome on a stone toadstool in some suburban garden. At the same time he bore some resemblance to a bad self-portrait by Van Gogh. He had a rather matted, dank appearance. He looked as if he had just returned from spending an uncomfortable night in a very dark cave, hiding, perhaps, in the

---

*Harcourt Brace published the first volume in 1933, a tedious and stuffy book lacking the swift, sure excitement of her portrait of Lawrence in her *Lorenzo in Taos* (republished in 1980 by Knopf).

> darkness from something which, at the same
> time, he on his side was hunting.

Lawrence appeared to be gravely ill, as if the flame of him had been quenched—this must have been the aftermath of his malarial attack. He tried to create the impression (according to Edith Sitwell) that he was a son of the soil and seemed to be baiting them by contrasting his childhood to their more affluent one. "This was not our fault," writes Dame Edith. "Our childhood was hell, and we refused to be discomforted." Frieda explained the natives of Bloomsbury to the Sitwells and told Dame Edith how she was obliged to protect Lawrence from the snares they set for him. Nonetheless, Dame Edith remarks, "The couple can never have a dull moment, since everyone who met them fell in love with either Mr. or Mrs. Lawrence." The Sitwells had to leave before they themselves could develop such affirmative feelings.

But once the weather became kindly again, Lawrence overcame his melancholia. "It's summer here, and all the cistus, white and pink, wide out in the wood—and fireflies by night, the uncertain sparky sort. . . . We are in the thick of good fat asparagus, and peas, and beans, and *carciofi* [artichokes]: and the peasants brought us a basket of first cherries on Saturday. So quickly the time goes by!" he writes to Aldington. About this time he must have gone on those walking tours of Tuscany which Millicent Beveridge describes to Catherine Carswell. As they tramped through the hilly terrain, Lawrence pointed out to her and discoursed upon at least thirty varieties of wild flowers and plants. Out of these walks Lawrence fashioned that fragrant, joyous essay called "Flowery Tuscany," first published serially in the *New Criterion* of 1927 (not to be confused with T. S. Eliot's *Criterion*) and later collected in *Phoenix*.

It must have been about this time that Lawrence wrote his

introduction to Mary Steegmann's translation of *The Mother* by Grazia Deledda (reprinted in *Phoenix*). Lawrence's interest in the great Sardinian writer is recorded as early as December of 1916, when he asks Koteliansky to buy him her novels from the Italian library at Charing Cross. Two years later, he tells Katherine Mansfield that Deledda is "very interesting," better than D'Annunzio, and in *Sea and Sardinia*, he mentions a visit to what he thought was the house where she had lived before she moved to Rome. Thus, when Deledda was awarded the Nobel Prize for Literature in 1926, Lawrence was ready and willing to write an appreciation of the English version that Jonathan Cape was preparing to publish the following year (1928). This novel, with its absorption in "the passionate complex of a primitive populace," brought back memories of his trip through what he calls, in the introduction, "one of the wildest, remotest parts of Europe, with a strange people and a mysterious past of its own."

Shortly after this labor of love was completed, Christine Hughes and her daughter Mary, both recovering from minor injuries sustained in an automobile accident, visited Lawrence for a few days and behaved idiotically. On June 9, 1927, he writes to Brewster:

> Really, *nothing* is worse than these Americans. They've cut out *everything* except personal conceit and clothes. I was in the Uffizi—Ufizzi— Uffizzi?—with them yesterday.—'My, look what awful hands she's got!' is all that comes out of Mary Christine for Lippo Lippi—they've never even heard of Botticelli . . . Standing in the Piazza Signoria I say—There's that Michelangelo 'David'—and they reply: Which one is it then?—that one at the end?—meaning the

> Bandinelli . . . They simply *can't* see anything:
> you might as well ask a dog to look at a picture
> or a statue. They're stone blind, culturally.

Lawrence exacted handsome revenge by making Mary Christine the target of an uncharitable limerick and of possibly a long, nasty poem, "So There!"

Almost on the heels of the Hugheses, Maria Huxley visited the Lawrences, accompanied by Barone Luigi Franchetti ("rich as Croesus . . . plays the piano well") and his wife Yvonne Paravicini Franchetti, the daughter of a Florentine father and an English mother. During the conversation over tea, Lawrence apparently made some remarks about Catherine Carswell ("That damned Catherine hasn't sent me any typing etc. But nothing malicious, why should I?") that his guests misunderstood but remembered to repeat to Mrs. Carswell later on in London—causing a brief breach which Lawrence had to repair with conciliatory letters. Before leaving, Maria invited the Lawrences to spend a few days with her and Aldous at Forte dei Marmi, a bathing resort not far from the Lerici that Lawrence still recalled fondly. The Franchettis, who owned a villa there, must have added their voices to the invitation.

The Lawrences went, but none of the old Ligurian magic was there: Forte dei Marmi was "beastly as a place . . . flat, dead sea, jelly fishy, and millions of villas." The Lawrences and the Huxleys motored back by way of the magnificent little city of Lucca, and that evening after an outdoor supper at the Villa Mirenda, they went into Florence for the feast of San Giovanni. Sitting in the Huxleys' car, they watched the fireworks light up the summer sky as the spectators jammed the Lungarno—an occasion that Lawrence was to describe in "Fireworks in Florence," a gem of an essay which should be read in conjunction with another one called "David" and the

chapter in *Aaron's Rod* called "Florence." Together they form
an eloquent triptych of tribute to that city.

Lawrence thought about making a swing through the
"secondary" Etruscan cities, this time with Frieda, but in July
he came down with a "bronchial hemorrhage." This one confined him to bed for eight days before Frieda, with the assis-
tance of Giulia and the other peasants, was able to nurse him
back to a semblance of health. His physician, Professor Giglioli, "the best doctor in Florence," would rush up to the
Mirenda at dusk, calm the jittery Frieda "like Jesus on the
waters," and treat Lawrence with "an abominable medicine"
called Coagulina. He advised Lawrence to avail himself of
the dry, clear air of the mountains and cautioned him "not to
take sea-baths" as he had been doing at Forte dei Marmi.
Visits from Orioli and the Huxleys helped to ease his
convalescence.

When Lawrence felt well enough again, he finished the
painting of the Resurrection and pushed forward with
the Etruscan sketches, even though he was convinced that the
book would be "a piece of hopeless popularity." He became
absorbed in a volume called *The Apocalypse Unveiled*, which
intensified his interest in Yoga and mysticism, an interest he
was to develop in a book of his own bearing a similar title. By
the middle of the summer, he was strong enough to resume
some of his relationships with his circle of acquaintances in
Florence. He would spend an occasional afternoon in Orioli's
bookshop, talking to Pino and his assistant Carlo Zanotti
(apparently the possibility of a private printing of *Lady Chatterley* had already come up between them), and during the
evenings, Orioli would come to Scandicci and drink Gancia
with Lawrence on the balcony of the villa. Sometimes Lawrence would join a group of Florentine intellectuals and
artists at their favorite restaurant at the Piazza Cavour.
Among them were Dr. Carlo Fasola and his daughter Con-

stanza, who was married to a man named Petterich.*
Dr. Fasola had been a professor of German literature at the
University of Florence until he had been dismissed for "pro-
German sympathies." He and his family were drawn to the
thin, red-bearded writer and his German wife, who had suffered similar indignities in England. According to the daughter of Constanza, now married to the physician Dr. Mario
Nepi, the Lawrences and the Petterichs saw each other with
some frequency—Constanza had the Lawrences as guests
for a week at the family villa in Santa Margherita a Montier
(a suburb of Florence where the Nepis now live) and spent
some time with them at Forte dei Marmi in 1927 and 1929,
possibly as their host. It may have been at the Villa Fasola
that the Lawrences spent the Christmas of 1927 with the
Huxleys, who had been friendly with the Fasolas since 1921,
when they had rented a villa opposite them in Santa Margherita. Dr. Nepi recalls that his mother-in-law also spoke of
another member of the Piazza Cavour circle, a lawyer
named Giovanni Carrozza, who reputedly had in his possession some valuable Lawrence memorabilia. And it is worth
mentioning here that Constanza and her husband visited
Frieda at Vence one day soon after the death of Lawrence.
She showed them his clothes in the closet and said she felt as
though Lawrence were still alive, his body in the clothing.
Then they prepared sandwiches and had a picnic on Lawrence's grave that afternoon.

By midsummer of 1927, the damp, musty mornings followed by hot, still afternoons were apparently irritating
Lawrence's "bronchials" beyond bearing, and on August 14,
he and Frieda went into Florence and took the *wagon-lit* for

---

*This is the couple, I believe, that Edward Nehls is unable to identify in
his third volume of the composite biography. "Constanza" is Italian for
"Constance." Writing *Lady Chatterley*, Lawrence may have used her name
for his heroine.

Austria. On the following day, they were in Villach. They stayed at the Hotel Fischer for three weeks, and during this time, Lawrence worked on his translation of *Cavalleria Rusticana* on rainy days—his correspondence with Orioli is full of questions about the Sicilian anatomy—"when the *cavalla gonfiava le froge al pari di un mastino ringhioso*—which part of her precious self did she swell out?" From Villach, the Lawrences went to Salzburg in time for the Mozart Festival and the Max Reinhardt version of *Everyman* at the cathedral. They spent September at the summer cottage of Frieda's sister, where they earlier had passed some idyllic days together. During the next two weeks, they were in Baden-Baden, visiting Frieda's mother. From there Lawrence wrote to Alfred Knopf that he would "sweat around Arezzo and Chiusi and Orvieto," on another Etruscan tour, this time with Frieda, and do six more Etruscan sketches if Knopf liked the first six which had been sent to him. Knopf must have been cool to this idea, for Lawrence apparently made no effort to move in that direction after returning to Florence on October 20.

Perhaps because of the tender memories evoked by Irschenhausen, Lawrence found that Italy had become an unexpectedly depressing place. The fall mornings were misty and damp, and the hunters banging away from dawn to dusk in their seasonal slaughter of little birds made him feel that the Italians were stupid. And the political situation had become increasingly tense in the last year. In 1924, while preparing the Epilogue to the second edition of *Movements in European History*, Lawrence had described a Fascist attack on the mayor of Fiesole in the middle of the night: "The mayor was forced to get up and open the door. The Fascisti seized him, stood him against the wall of his house, and shot him under the eyes of his wife and children, who were in their night dresses. Why? Because he was a socialist. That is Fascism and Law and Order. Only another kind of bullying."

And now Lawrence was fed up with both fogs and fascism.* To the Huxleys, he confesses, "I'd like to clear out of Italy for good," and to another correspondent, he says, "I'm not happy here, and I don't know where else to go." India beckoned, but he did not have enough money to make the trip. A little house in Ireland, he thought, might rejuvenate his ambition, suffocating in Scandicci: ". . . how can I sit in this empty house and see nobody and do nothing?" he asks a friend. And of course Lawrence was ill, gravely ill.

But, as Catherine Carswell says, he proved his strength by refusing to become an invalid. He writes to Brewster: "I'm feeling really better—I'm better when I grumble—like my old grandmother, who was never anything but worse and fading fast, for forty years, till she was dying, at 75. . . . " Despite his illness and his isolation, he prepared the Etruscan essays for publication, wrote some stories and essays, polished some old poems for a new collection, and probably started the third and final version of *Lady Chatterley's Lover*. About this time, he did some more painting. Like *Lady Chatterley* and *Etruscan Places*, these canvases reflect an unquenchable spirit, almost a playful mood, especially the one called *Expulsion from Eden*, which shows Adam and Eve chasing God out of the Garden of Paradise. He thought it would be a lark to show these pictures in New York the next time he went to America.

By November, 1927, he had resumed an almost normal schedule of activities. He accompanied the Wilkinsons on a motor drive to San Gimignano, the medieval fortress town "with its towers rising above it like upright hair." Lawrence could work up no enthusiasm for the famous walled city— unlike most travelers, he loathed the "preserved pictur-

---

*Earlier, when Violet Gibson had tried to assassinate Mussolini and the bullet from her gun only punctured his nose, Lawrence said to Ravagli, "Put a ring through it." There is no evidence for the carelessly repeated charge that Lawrence was sympathetic to fascism.

esque." A day or so later, Reggie Turner, Pino Orioli, Charles Scott-Moncrieff (the translator of Proust), and Harold Acton appeared at the Mirenda. According to Acton, Lawrence was "gentle, polite, almost lady-like" to his guests as he proudly showed them his collection of paintings which decorated the walls of the sitting room. Lawrence poured tea and served Frieda's puddings while they "poured the rest."

On November 17, 1927, Lawrence ventured into Florence for the first time since his return to Mirenda. While walking down the Lungarno, he ran into Michael Arlen (Dikran Kouyoumdjian), looking "thinner, perhaps otherwise much the same" as in the Bloomsbury days when they had met at Lady Ottoline Morrell's. The Armenian novelist, whom Lawrence always addressed as "Dikran," had taken an apartment on the Borgo San Giorgio after undergoing a tubercular cure at Davos. Despite the wealth and popularity earned by *The Green Hat*, his novel about sexual license among the affluent, "the Florence snobs . . . who had made such a fuss of him" once were now cutting him dead. Lawrence immediately invited him out to the Mirenda. A few days later he sent a hasty message via the Wilkinsons to Orioli:

> Would you mind sending Carletto [Zanotti, his shop assistant] over to Michael Arlen with this note . . . He . . . was coming out on Wednesday—But Frieda's got a cold, in bed today, and Michael A. is terrified of getting a cold. So I must warn him.

Either Arlen's anxiety or Frieda's illness (or both) abated, for Arlen was at the Mirenda on the following Saturday, telling Lawrence that he had put all his American royalties into a trust fund that he couldn't touch until he became thirty-five. Lawrence, who had once scorned Arlen, now admired him and wrote to Richard Aldington: "He's one of the few people I don't mind making their pile—just to spite 'em." The *anima* of Arlen must have infiltrated his creative consciousness as he was working on a new novel and a long short story: both Michaelis, the successful writer in *Lady Chatterley* and Arnault, the powerful Armenian patriarch in "Mother and Daughter," seem to owe something to the figure of the Armenian immigrant who "made good."

In December of that year, the Carswells, no longer angry with Lawrence, invited him to spend Christmas with them in the Harz Mountains: a German lung specialist was keenly interested in his work and had offered to treat his insulted lungs without asking for a fee. But Lawrence by now was "tired to death crawling about and being driven to consult new doctors," and Frieda was reluctant to leave the place that had become home to her. They decided to stay on, and that Christmas Eve they again decorated a tree that Pietro had stolen from the woods, and with Lawrence singing carols, entertained the peasant children, who thought the tree was a miracle. On Christmas of 1927, the Wilkinsons paid a visit and the Huxleys drove Lawrence and Frieda to a friend's villa for the day.

Noting how constant his cough had become, the Huxleys persuaded Lawrence to fly the vagaries of another Tuscan winter. They were going to Les Diablerets in Switzerland and they would find a hotel room nearby for their friends. Lawrence, always averse to snow and icy mountains, wanted to try Egypt, but Dr. Giglioli advised him that the altitude of Les Diablerets would be much better than Cairo's for a cure.

However, Lawrence's departure was delayed, first by a racking cough that put him in bed for four days, then by Nelly Morrison's refusal to finish typing the final chapters of his new novel (which he had re-christened "Tenderness"). Hence, it was not until the end of January of 1928 that he was able to "creep up" with Frieda to the Swiss mountains and the welcome company of the Huxleys.

Though Lawrence did not relish the enforced inactivity of almost two months at the Chalet Beau Site, both his vitality and view of life improved in the bracing mountain air. First, he was cheered by seeing the final sketch of the six-part Etruscan series on the pages of *Travel*. And he found the necessary energy to prepare and send off an expurgated version of "Tenderness" ("it bleeds") to Laurence Pollinger, his agent at Curtis Brown (it was published in 1932 by Alfred Knopf as the "authorized abridged edition"). He then turned his attention to the third and final version, now complete in typescript. Juliette Huxley, Julian's wife, who read the completed manuscript and disapproved strongly of parts, told Lawrence "rather savagely" that the title might just as well have been "John Thomas and Lady Jane." Lawrence accepted her suggestion for the second version of the novel.*

At least two publishers, aware of the furor raised by *The Rainbow*, rejected the manuscript. Before it could go to another London house (Chatto), Lawrence asked Maria Huxley to pick up the typescript (she had typed half of it) from Curtis Brown and to remove it from circulation. Following the example of Norman Douglas, Lawrence decided to publish himself and to sell the book by subscription, a possibility he had been considering as early as November of the previous year.

Meanwhile, Orioli had been active in Lawrence's behalf. He knew a printer named Franceschini, who didn't read English and therefore could not object to Lawrence's language, as Nelly Morrison had ("Dirty bitch!" Lawrence called her). When the shop was ready to receive the manuscript, Lawrence left Les Diablerets early in March, met Frieda in Milan (she had gone to Baden for one of her family visits), and came down to a Florence covered with sleet, his mind brim-

---

*Published by Viking in 1972, by Mondadori (in Italian) in 1954. For an account of the tangled history of *Lady Chatterley*, see Warren Roberts, *A Bibliography of D. H. Lawrence*.

ming with excitement over the new venture. He would have given up the Mirenda that harsh spring, perhaps for the ranch in New Mexico, had he not been so determined to see his "tender phallic novel" through the press himself. Though type was scarce (it had to be pied and recast), paper in short supply, and English punctuation a total mystery at Tipografia Giuntina, he and Orioli pushed the project briskly ahead.

During this difficult printing—described amusingly in *A Propos of Lady Chatterley's Lover*—Lawrence fell ill again, the pain of bronchial hemorrhages aggravated by an infected molar. This time Frieda was not present to nurse him—she had gone up to Alassio to visit Barbara—but Pino Orioli attended to his needs, bringing food and other necessities from Florence and often staying with him so that he would not be alone. However, even before Frieda had returned, Lawrence was back on his feet, reading the proofs of *Lady Chatterley* (the printer wrote "dind't, didn'nt, dnid't, dind't, din'dt, didn't like a Bach fugue," Lawrence complained) not always aware that the Italian printers had to contend with his crabbed handwriting in an alien language as they readied the thousand copies that were to be sold through subscription for two pounds each.

The day after Frieda got back (April 16), Lawrence was feeling well enough to take her into Florence for lunch with the Waterfields, their old friends from Aulla who had inherited a villa in the Tuscan hills. They were joined by Lady Sybil Colefax, whom he had met during his Bloomsbury days at Garsington. Lawrence liked Lady Colefax and invited her for tea at the Mirenda. She came twice during late April, and though (according to Lawrence), she acted as if "he would bite," she apparently ordered five copies of *Lady Chatterley*, still in proof at the printer's.

With the new novel soon coming off the press, volunteers helped with the distribution. In May, when Enid Hilton, the daughter of Lawrence's old Eastwood friend, Will Hopkin,

arrived in Scandicci with her husband for a two weeks' holiday, the two of them were given the task of sending out
announcements and urging friends to advertise its availabil-
ity. Among his other friends who acted as agents for the
distribution of it were the Huxleys, Harriet Monroe, Witter
Bynner, Rolf Gardiner, and Harry Crosby.

It may have been this publicity about the imminent
appearance of a new novel by one of the world's great living
writers that prompted visits by two men in the American
publishing world. One of them, Robert H. Davis, an editor
and writer, came to Orioli's bookshop on the Lungarno Cor-
sini and worshipfully photographed Lawrence. The pictures,
which Frieda thought were very good likenesses, would
appear in Davis's book, *Man Makes His Own Masks* (1932). A
little later on, Bennett Cerf, accompanied by Norman Douglas and possibly Earl Brewster, called at the Villa Mirenda,
perhaps with the idea of signing Lawrence to a contract.
Lawrence and Douglas, says Cerf, greeted one another in a
friendly fashion, but as soon as they were alone, Lawrence
asked Cerf what he meant by bringing such a man to the
Villa Mirenda. It is possible that Lawrence may have been
chaffing his American visitor, for he had patched up his
differences with Douglas just two and a half months before.

It was Pino Orioli, according to Richard Aldington, who
had been responsible for this reconcilation. After making
each acknowledge his sins, Orioli brought them together in
his bookshop on March 26 (1928). Lawrence and Frieda were
talking to Orioli when in walked Douglas as arranged. There
was an "embarrassed silence." Then Douglas offered Lawrence his snuffbox and said, "Have a pinch of snuff, dearie."
Lawrence took it. "Isn't it curious," he said—sniff—"only
Norman and father ever"—sniff—"gave me snuff." Lawrence later reported to Huxley that their now mutual friend
looked aged and longed to visit Aleppo by Orient Express.
"From Aleppo he wants to go to Baalbek and then presum-

ably, to rise into heaven." Douglas went to none of those places probably, but the following year, he did go to Bandol and have a final cognac with Lawrence.

Sometime during the spring of 1928, Lawrence had played host to Margaret Gardiner, the sister of Rolf Gardiner, an English writer, who had made a pilgrimage to Les Diablerets two years earlier. As Lawrence was shepherding the young schoolteacher around the house, they were joined by two spinsters of whom he seemed to be inordinately fond, though behind their backs he was calling them "The Virgins" (Harry Moore believes that they may have been Millicent Beveridge and her friend Mabel Harrison, with whom Lawrence had hiked on Sorrento). When Lawrence showed them his latest paintings, they expressed disapproval of the canvas of a man urinating (*Dandelions*) and also of his *Holy Family*, with its bare-breasted Mary and its sensual, Italianate Joseph, together eclipsing a vacant-faced adolescent Christ. And when they saw his illustrations for a Boccaccio story, they wondered aloud why he had to insert among the proper nuns a sleeping gardener with his penis exposed. Later, alone with Miss Gardiner, Lawrence read her the indignant reactions of the *Forum* readers to "The Escaped Cock," commenting freely on the state of their intelligence.

In late May or early June, *Lady Chatterley* finally came off the press. Lawrence was delighted with its appearance, "a handsome and dignified volume," with a terra-cotta cover that bore his emblem, a black phoenix rising from its nest in flames. (The original of the emblem, in Lawrence's own hand, was in the possession of Caresse Crosby before her death.*) Enid Hilton took two copies which she wanted to smuggle in her knickers past the English censors and Frieda,

---

*Curiously enough, even the emblem of the phoenix may have been derived from an Italian source. As Lawrence designed the emblem, the firebird sits in an urnlike receptacle. In the seventeenth century, there was a

after contemplating the copies piled high in the printer's shop, exclaimed, "We shall never sell all these!"†

In June of 1928, Lawrence wound up his business in Florence (the mailing of the books was to be taken care of by Orioli), and he was preparing to leave the Villa Mirenda for good. He intended to take a small place in the French or Swiss Alps for the summer, and then perhaps find a place to settle down again on the Mediterranean. As he began to pack his paintings and his trunks, Frieda was so saddened by the scene that Lawrence decided to lease the villa for an additional six months. Since the Brewsters were coming to Scandicci to search for a place, he offered it to them for the summer.

When the Brewsters arrived at the Villa Mirenda, seriously considering the proposal, they were shocked by Lawrence's appearance. His jaunty garb of white flannels and flax-blue blazer failed to hide the serious nature of his illness. In recalling that visit, Achsah Brewster writes, "We

---

network of *botteghe* all of which were named *Libreria della Fenice*. This chain-store enterprise maintained branches in all of the large cities of northern Italy. The publisher, Giovanni Gabriele Giolito, illustrated an edition of Petrarch (no doubt available in the antiquarian Florentine bookstores that Lawrence frequented) with the emblematic design of a phoenix celebrating the amatory oneness of the lovers shown on the urn.

The entire fall 1972 issue of *The D. H. Lawrence Review* is devoted to the phoenix as an emblem, but as far as I could tell, the Giolito phoenix, the one most likely to be familiar to Lawrence at the time, is not mentioned.

Perhaps the first occurrence of the image in his fiction we find in *Aaron's Rod*: "She was . . . throwing cold water over his phoenix newly risen from the ashes of its nest in flames." When Tennessee Williams wrote his one-act play about the last days of Lawrence, he took his title from that passage: *I Rise in Flames, Cried the Phoenix*.

†Even with pirated editions proliferating in the wake of the original, nearly all the copies were sold and the venture was to net Lawrence a decent profit of 1616 pounds, most of which, Richard Aldington says, he lost in the stock-market crash of 1929.

knew that we must not postpone to the future our time with him, but to seize each passing day." Instead of staying behind in Scandicci, they decided to accompany the Lawrences to their destination.

After a gay farewell luncheon on June 10, they caught the Pisa–Genoa–Turin train while still in a holiday mood. As their compartment gradually emptied of passengers, they began to sing revivalist hymns and Salvation Army songs, one after the other. The climax came when Lawrence arose during the rendition of "Throw Out the Life-Line," tossed out an imaginary lasso, and hauled in imaginary drowning souls. That evening they stayed in Turin, and on the following day they began a leisurely motor tour of the Alps. At a rustic, flowery inn near Grenoble, where they thought they might stay for a while, Lawrence coughed all night. In the morning, the proprietor told Earl Brewster that it was against the law for him to accommodate a man with infected lungs. Brewster tactfully moved the party to the Grand Hotel at Chexbres-sur-Vevey overlooking Lake Leman. Here Lawrence wrote several of the articles that were to be published under the title of *Assorted Articles*, and here, too, amid great excitement, he opened the package containing the author's copies of *Lady Chatterley's Lover*.

After a restorative month at Chexbres-sur-Vevey, the Lawrences, longing for a place of their own, found a little peasant chalet above the village of Gsteig-bei-Gstaad, not far from Bern, and decided to spend the summer there. Lawrence lacked the strength to climb the slopes or walk at length, but he occupied himself energetically with writing and making arrangements for the exhibition of his paintings at the Warren Gallery in London. He wrote "The Flying Fish," "Cocksure Women and Hensure Men," and the second part of "The Escaped Cock" (the first half had already appeared in *The Forum*). He made arrangements to publish the Italian story called "Sun" with Harry Crosby's Black Sun

Press and he instructed Orioli to put *Lady Chatterley* in false
dust-jackets—it was to be advertised as *The Way of All Flesh*.
He remained at Gsteig until he could no longer endure the
"beastly climate, hot and cold at once," and on September 18
(1928) he and Frieda once more sought the sanctuary of
Baden-Baden.

Frieda was going down to Florence to close up the Villa
Mirenda and to finish some odd packing; it apparently
crossed Lawrence's mind to accompany her, but the Mirendas had dismissed Giulia and Pietro Pini, and Lawrence did
not feel up to facing the house without help. Frieda went by
herself while Lawrence waited for her at Le Lavandou, on
the French Riviera. When Frieda arrived after an absence of
about a week ("business" had required her to go to Trieste,
where Angelo Ravagli was stationed), she had a "raging Italian cold" which she passed on to Lawrence. It later developed
into flu, but Lawrence was too excited to stay in bed. Instead
he and Frieda visited Richard Aldington, who had rented
Jean Paulhan's comfortable little cottage, La Vignie, on the
nearby island of Port-Cros. They were treated hospitably by
the Aldingtons, even when Lawrence, now more gravely ill
than ever, kept the household awake all night with his
"dreadful hollow cough." On warm days he chipped away at
his translation of *The Story of Dr. Manente*, by the sixteenth-
century Florentine apothecary and author, Anton Grazzini,
known as Il Lasca (the Roach), from his bed, calling out to
Aldington for advice about how to capture the sense of
Grazzini's racy wit—could one use the word "tithe" for
catasto or was it more exactly "tax"? While Brigit Patmore,
the Irish writer who had married Deighton Patmore, the
grandson of Coventry Patmore, typed the manuscript of the
translation, he told her that he had eight hundred pounds
from *Lady Chatterley* and that he wanted to take a villa, with a
butler, at Taormina, and live like a gentleman. Perhaps he

had been made homesick for the south by the presence of a
Sicilian servant named Giuseppe, "a strong fellow of 28,"
who fetched all the provisions on a donkey once a day and in
general reminded Lawrence of the pleasant, courteous,
hardworking peasants of the Fontana Vecchia days.

The Ile de Port-Cros in winter had its drawbacks: there
was no medical service available, and when it stormed (frequently), the boat from the mainland with the daily provisions could not make the crossing. This rather rugged life,
which once might have delighted a healthy Lawrence, now
irritated his cough-wracked shadow, and he persuaded
Frieda to try Bandol, at least long enough for them to gather
their wits and to determine where they would go next.
Frieda was "fidgety wanting a place of her own to spread out
in," but where she didn't know—she oscillated between Lago
di Garda and Taormina. Though Lawrence wanted to see
Spain, his instinct was to go south (Garda, he thought,
would be too cold) to the sun of Italy, to a place whose spirit
might infuse the final pages of the Etruscan book. Lawrence
complained that "blank indecision" kept them anchored at
the Hotel Beau Rivage in Bandol, but the sight of the fishermen bringing in their daily catch, "the sea swimming with
milky golden light at sunset," the clear, starry skies in the
cool evenings, must have awakened tender memories and
must have played a part in holding the Lawrences there for
almost four months.

During that time, Lawrence collected his latest poems into
a volume called *Pansies* and sent them to his London publisher. As they came through the mail, the British authorities seized the manuscript copies, and only after fourteen of
the offending poems were removed could the collection be
published that July in England (later, Lawrence brought out
a private edition with the missing poems restored). The
relative success of *Lady Chatterley* led Lawrence to suggest

another publishing idea to Orioli which he felt sure would be profitable. It was to be a series of stories by Italian Renaissance writers translated and introduced by such writers as Aldous Huxley and Norman Douglas. Before Orioli had approved of the plan, Lawrence had been plodding along with the translation of *The Story of Dr. Manente*.

If Orioli can be trusted, Lawrence must have been in Florence sometime during February of 1929, although no other evidence sustains this supposition. *The Story of Dr. Manente* appeared in March of 1929. According to Orioli's account to Aldington, Lawrence wrote the whole of the introduction at his bookshop on Lungarno. He was dissatisfied with the introduction written by Orioli's "old professor" (possibly Carlo Fasola), and produced his own, "quite indifferent to the people coming in and out of the shop and all the resonant Italian voices."

Near the end of March, the Lawrences were in Paris again on business, arranging for the publication of the story "Sun" with Harry Crosby and working out terms with Edward Titus for an unexpurgated paperback edition of "Our Lady" (as the Lawrences had by now christened the novel) intended to outflank the pirates who were profiting from his book. When these matters were concluded, they must have enjoyed the Parisian spring in the company of the Huxleys and the Crosbys (at least Caresse Crosby thought so).

In April, Lawrence and Frieda drifted down through southern France and Spain to Majorca. Lawrence liked the loveliness of the island, which reminded him of Sicily, but when Frieda refused to learn a word of Spanish, Lawrence wondered whether Italy after all might not be the best place for them to live. And as he got to know the "rancid" Balearic natives, he concluded that the Italians by comparison were "more alive, more frank, more life-generous." Frieda was "again moaning for a house," and Lawrence decided that while Frieda was away, he would search for one on Lago di Garda or in Marina di Massa, not far from the place where they had lived so happily fifteen years earlier.

At the beginning of the summer, Frieda went up to England to see her children and to arrange for the publication of the book of Lawrence's pictures while Lawrence looked around Marina di Massa for a little villa. He found nothing that suited him and continued down the coast to the neighboring town of Forte dei Marmi, where the Huxleys were again spending their vacation in a house they had rented from the Fasolas. Lawrence took a room in a *pensione* called the Giuliani for all or most of his stay. This time he had fewer complaints about Forte dei Marmi. His quarters were comfortable and inexpensive, and there was a maid of all work who brought breakfast to his bedside and served him lunch in the shaded garden separated from the Fasola house by a pomegranate hedge. Frieda's absence was balanced by the presence of a young American admirer named Maria Cristina Chambers, who apparently was his guest at the *pensione* for two weeks. He introduced her to Pino Orioli ("he rescued our *Lady* from oblivion"), to the Huxleys, the Petterichs, Yvonne Franchetti ("very *cattive* with M.C. [Maria Chambers]"), Nelly Morrison, a Signore Sansani, the American friend from Palermo, and no doubt others who provided company and distraction from his personal pain and publishing woes. He told Maria Cristina* that Mark Rampion, of *Point Counter*

---

*Maria Cristina Chambers, the wife of the editor of *The Literary Digest*, worshiped Lawrence from afar, and when she announced that she was going to visit him at Forte dei Marmi, Lawrence agreed to put her up. Frieda says that he dreaded her presence because the emotional strain was too much for him. Perhaps Maria Huxley and Yvonne Franchetti were *cattive* with her because they sensed something of an emotional imposition on the fragile Lawrence.

Point, was a "very bad" version of him. He would walk along the seashore and often lounge on the beach with her and the Huxleys at their "favorite spot." Perhaps because he himself had been forbidden to bathe by his physician, he abhorred even more than usual the spectacle of "blatant bathers" sunning themselves like seals—"all terribly aware of *themselves* and their beastly bodies." It must have been there that he composed in his mind those barbed poems "Forte dei Marmi," "Sea Bathers," and "The Gods! The Gods!" (*More Pansies*).

He and Huxley painted together, and once Maria Huxley posed for her husband in the nude. She later confessed to Lawrence that she hadn't liked doing it because she got cold lying on the bed as her husband squinted at her figure.

From London, Frieda sent word that the exhibition of Lawrence's paintings had opened at the Warren Gallery at 39a Maddox Street on June 15. Many of the twenty-five paintings there owed their presence to the efforts of Enid and Laurence Hilton. The summer before, the Hiltons had carted away from the Villa Mirenda a number of paintings and watercolors, disguised with false fronts of classical reproductions, back to Eastwood and had stored them there under a bed until the time of the exhibition. Seventeen of the paintings were sold in less than three weeks, and according to Frieda, interest in them remained high.

Further sales seemed likely, until the police visited the exhibition on July 5, one day before the exhibition would have closed, and carried off thirteen of the twenty-five works as obscene, to be sequestered and held in custody until after a hearing at Great Marlborough Street on August 8. However—and on this point Aldington, Moore, and other biographers appear to be in error—the exhibition was never closed down. Dorothy Warren refused to close it, and according to her husband, Philip Coutts Trotter, she replenished the exhibition during July with eight early Lawrence paintings, and the show continued until after August 8, making it the second longest to be held at the Warren Gallery. What brought about the closing was not the police visit, but a notice of dangerous structure served by the London County Council on the proprietors of the gallery.*

In early July, Lawrence bought a new trunk, packed it with meticulous care (he corrected the way Maria Cristina folded one of his coats at least three times), and prepared to leave Forte dei Marmi by train. Since Frieda was in London visiting her children, he had planned to stop over at Orioli's in Florence before going up to Lake Como for another brief holiday. His letters convey the impression that he was in good health and robust spirits, but Aldous Huxley, writing to Robert Nichols shortly after Lawrence's departure, says: "D. H. Lawrence was here [Forte dei Marmi] for a little . . . How horrible [his] gradually approaching dissolution is— and in this case, specially horrible because so unnecessary." Indeed Mariuccia the maid told Maria Cristina that once he had coughed all during the night. Lawrence says in a letter that he had a "bad cold in my legs and lower man" while Richard Aldington says that he had an upset stomach similar to the one he had suffered in Mexico. Whatever he had, he was ill and had to be driven over to Orioli's apartment in Florence by Maria Huxley.

After she deposited him at Orioli's, the fit of coughing recurred. Lawrence pretended that he had nothing more

---

*"The perverse legend" that the police "authorities" closed the exhibition sprang into existence on March 4, 1930, in an erroneous obituary notice about Lawrence, according to Philip Trotter, and, he says, has persisted ever since.

than a "misery" caused by sitting too late on the beach one afternoon, but Orioli, fearing the worst, summoned Frieda by cable and set about to nursing his patient.* During his illness, as he lay in bed "with head and arms hanging limply over the side, looking . . . like an old picture of the Descent from the Cross," Lawrence received word that the London police allegedly intended to burn his canvases to a crisp. "*Auto-da-fé!*" he fumed, too sick to lift his head off the pillow. But Orioli's devotion and the prospect that Frieda would soon appear pulled him through the illness. When Frieda did arrive, he was already dressing himself and talking about departure. When Lawrence first fell ill, Orioli had asked him, "What will Frieda say when she arrives?" Lawrence had answered, "Do you see those peaches in the bowl? She will say, 'What lovely peaches' and she will devour them." Now, as Frieda realized that Lawrence was out of danger, she felt thirsty from the long journey and she ate the peaches.

Lawrence's rally was, in the phrase of Philip Trotter, "brief but spectacular." With Frieda's help, he moved out of the crowded apartment to the Hotel Porta Rossa, from where they could see the tower of the Piazza della Signora, where Aaron Sisson had wandered wide-eyed some years before. During their stay there (it must have been for several days), Lawrence wrote some of the poems in *Nettles* and apparently spent one or two days wandering around Scan-

---

*In *Adventures of a Bookseller*, Orioli recalls this episode as "the reverse" of the few golden moments he had with Lawrence. In matters of business, Lawrence was "troublesome" and as a friend disappointing and disheartening, he says.

Despite such recollections in untranquillity, Orioli could write to Maria Cristina Chambers after Lawrence's death: "We shall never see him again and we shall never hear his soft, soothing voice, or see his blue eyes looking into the soul of people he was fond of," and a few months later, "I have been twice to see Frieda at Vence, and Lorenzo's grave [he was probably with the Petterichs at the picnic]. We have put up on his grave a mosaic phoenix and planted roses all around."

dicci. To Lawrence it seemed "familiar and friendly," but Italy had gone "very flat" for him, "like a deflated tire." Before leaving for Baden-Baden, he and Frieda invited Orioli and Norman Douglas for a farewell luncheon. According to Douglas, they ordered and consumed the "largest fish he ever saw." In the rush to the train station, Douglas was left to pick up the bill.* "As the train moved out I thought to detect," writes Douglas, ". . . the phantom of a smile creeping over his wan face."

Later, at Bandol, when he could gaze out over the Mediterranean that he had always loved so much, he yearned to return south, especially to Sicily or to the Riviera di Levante so he could be near the Huxleys at Forte dei Marmi. But as he admits to Maria Cristina Chambers in a letter of January 21, 1930, he was too tired to move even his hand ("I can't write letters any more—and Frieda won't write them"), and thereafter until his death on March 2 of 1930, Italy existed for him only in his memories.

His affection for Italy remained one of his constant attachments in a life of restless, often dissatisfied wandering. There was only one break in this attachment, when the lure of America became too strong to ignore. His feelings are summed up by a statement in *Sea and Sardinia*: "Italy has given me back I know not what of myself, but a very, very great deal. She has found for me so much that was lost." After Lawrence himself, no one has described his attachment to that land better than his friend Catherine Carswell:

> Lawrence had loved Italy as much as any En-
> glish poet ever did, and he got from it more
> than most. He was grateful till the end of his
> life for that carelessness of the South which

---

*Douglas had managed once to make Lawrence pay for some drinks and suspected that Lawrence would be laying for revenge.

dispelled like an unconscious benison the harsh and petty carefulness of his Northern upbringing. Travelling north would always make him feel ill and resentful. Turning south would always offer ease and a healing. "It cures one of caring, and a good thing, too!" He felt that at the beginning and returned to it at the end.

Selected Bibliography

Letters

The Collected Letters. Edited by Harry Moore. Two vols. New York: Viking, 1962. London: Heinemann, 1962.
The Letters. Edited by Aldous Huxley. New York: Viking, 1932. London: Heinemann, 1932.
Letters to Bertrand Russell. Edited by Harry Moore. New York: Gotham Book Mart, 1948.
Lawrence in Love. Edited by James T. Boulton. Nottingham: Nottingham University Press, 1968.
The Quest for Rananim. Edited by George Zytaruk. McGill-Queens University Press, 1970.
The Centaur Letters. Austin: University of Texas Press, 1970.
The Selected Letters. Edited by Diana Trilling. New York: Anchor, 1961.
Letters to Martin Secker, 1911–1930. London: Privately printed, 1970.
D. H. Lawrence's Letters to Thomas and Adele Seltzer. Edited by Gerald M. Lacy. Santa Barbara: Black Sparrow Press, 1976.
The Letters of D. H. Lawrence, Vol I, 1901–1913. Edited by James T. Boulton. New York: Cambridge University Press, 1976.

Biographical and Critical Works

Aldington, Richard, *D. H. Lawrence: Portrait of a Genius. But . . . .* New York: Duell, Sloan, and Pearce, 1950.
Asquith, Lady Cynthia. *Diaries 1915–1918*. London: Hutchinson, 1968.

Brett, Dorothy. *Lawrence and Brett: A Friendship*. Philadelphia: Lippincott, 1933.

Brewster, Earl, and Brewster, Achsah. *D. H. Lawrence: Reminiscences and Correspondence*. London: Secker, 1934.

Carswell, Catherine. *The Savage Pilgrimage*. London: Secker, 1951 (revised edition).

Corsani, Mary. *D. H. Lawrence E L'Italia*. Milan: Mursia & Co., 1965.

Crosby, Caresse. *The Passionate Years*. Carbondale: Southern Illinois University Press, 1953.

Darroch, Sandra Jobson. *Ottoline*. New York: Coward, McCann & Geoghegan, 1975.

Delavenay, Emile. *D. H. Lawrence: The Man and His Work*. London: Heinemann, 1972.

Ford, Ford Madox (Hueffer). *Portraits from Life*. Boston: Houghton Mifflin, 1937.

Foster, Joseph. *D. H. Lawrence in Taos*. Albuquerque: University of New Mexico Press, 1972.

Gilles, Daniel, *D. H. Lawrence ou le Puritan Scandaleux*. Paris: Julliard, 1964.

Green, Martin. *The Von Richthofen Sisters*. New York: Basic Books, 1974.

Lawrence, Ada, and Gelder, G. Stuart. *Young Lorenzo: The Early Life of D. H. Lawrence*. London: Secker, 1932.

Lawrence, Frieda. *The Memoirs and Correspondence*. Edited by E. W. Tedlock. London: Heinemann, 1961.

————. *"Not I, But the Wind..."* New York: Viking, 1934.

Levy, Mervyn, editor. *The Paintings of D. H. Lawrence*. New York: Viking, 1964.

Lucas, Robert. *Frieda Lawrence*. New York: Viking, 1973. London: Secker & Warburg, 1973.

Luhan, Mabel Dodge. *Lorenzo in Taos*. New York: Alfred Knopf, 1932.

Mackenzie, Compton. *My Life and Times: Octave Five*. London: Chatto and Windus, 1966.

Moore, Harry. *The Priest of Love* (original title *The Intelligent Heart*). Carbondale: Southern Illinois University Press, 1979. London: Heinemann, 1974.

————. *Poste Restante: A Lawrence Travel Calendar.* With an Introduction by Mark Schorer. Berkeley: University of California
Press, 1956.

————, editor. *A D. H. Lawrence Miscellany.* Carbondale: Southern Illinois University Press, 1959.

Nehls, Edward, editor. *D. H. Lawrence. A Composite Biography.*
Three vols. Madison: University of Wisconsin Press, 1957–59.

Nin, Anaïs. *D. H. Lawrence: An Unprofessional Study.* Paris: E. W.
Titus, 1932.

Pinto, Vivian de Sola. *D. H. Lawrence: Prophet of the Midlands.*
Nottingham: University of Nottingham Press, 1951.

————, editor. *D. H. Lawrence After Thirty Years, 1930–1960.* Nottingham: Curwen Press, 1960.

Powell, Lawrence Clark. *The Manuscripts of D. H. Lawrence.* Los
Angeles Public Library, 1937.

Roberts, Warren. *A Bibliography of D. H. Lawrence.* London:
Rupert Hart-Davis, 1963.

Russell, Bertrand. *Portraits from Memory.* New York: Simon &
Schuster, 1956.

Sagar, Keith. *The Life of D. H. Lawrence.* New York: Pantheon,
1980.

Waterfield, Lena. *Castle in Italy.* London: John Murray, 1961.

Weintraub, Stanley. *Reggie.* New York: George Braziller, 1964.

West, Rebecca. *Ending in Earnest: A Literary Log.* New York:
Doubleday, Doran and Co., 1931.

Index